Essentials of Essay Writing

Essentials of Essay Writing

What Markers Look For

Jamie Q Roberts

 macmillan education · palgrave

© Jamie Q Roberts 2017

First published 2017 by
PALGRAVE

Palgrave in the UK is an imprint of Macmillan Publishers Limited, registered in England, company number 785998, of 4 Crinan Street, London, N1 9XW.

Palgrave® and Macmillan® are registered trademarks in the United States, the United Kingdom, Europe and other countries.

ISBN 978–1–137–57584–5 paperback

This book is printed on paper suitable for recycling and made from fully managed and sustained forest sources. Logging, pulping and manufacturing processes are expected to conform to the environmental regulations of the country of origin.

A catalogue record for this book is available from the British Library.

A catalog record for this book is available from the Library of Congress.

Contents

Acknowledgements

First and foremost, I want to thank the thousand or more students who have written essays and other assignments for my courses over the past 10 years. So much of what I now know about writing has come from evaluating your work. However, having the opportunity to mark is only half the story. I have been fortunate to have done most of my teaching at the Learning Centre at UNSW Australia, where the marking process is valued and ample time is allocated, and indeed, where writing abundant comments is encouraged. Sue Starfield and Dominic Fitzsimmons deserve a mention here. I have also benefited from the numerous conversations I have had with all my colleagues at the Learning Centre.

My thanks also extends to everyone who gave me permission to use their essays for this book. I am particularly grateful to the University of Warwick for granting permission to use extracts from the British Academic Written English (corpus). The corpus was developed at the Universities of Warwick, Reading and Oxford Brookes under the directorship of Hilary Nesi and Sheena Gardner (formerly of the Centre for Applied Linguistics, Warwick), Paul Thompson (formerly of the Department of Applied Linguistics, Reading) and Paul Wickens (School of Education, Oxford Brookes), with funding from the ESRC (RES-000-23-0800). It is one thing to learn from your own students, who tend to write the way you encourage them to write, it is another thing to learn from someone else's students. I am also grateful to all of the universities who gave me permission to draw upon their marking criteria. It was wonderful to see what people from different institutions and countries look for in essays and other assignments. I was glad to learn that we are all more or less on the same page.

Special thanks goes to Caitlin Hamilton and Yvette Selim who provided invaluable support in the early stages of producing this book; in difficult times you helped me get over the line. Thanks to Tracey-Lee Downey who helped with the design of the book. Thanks again to Sue Starfield, the director of the Learning Centre, who has always strongly supported this book. I am also immensely grateful for the ongoing support and guidance provided by Helen Caunce at Palgrave; it has been a pleasure working with you. Extra special thanks to my wife, Laura Fisher. On many a Saturday did you entertain our wonderful son, Max, while I slunk off to the office to write. We always said we would support each other, and we have! To my parents, Michael and Gillian, I guess you did something right. Finally, I thank the teachers who inspired me, both in the flesh and in particular on the page – I must mention Conrad, Nietzsche and Sterne. In the end it is your passion and integrity that made all the difference.

Introduction

What is a university essay and why does it exist?

Early in my undergraduate studies I thought that essays were mystical things that only a chosen few could craft. I certainly did not consider myself to be one of the chosen. Once, in a second year Philosophy course, I surprised myself by producing a strong essay, but it took me three more years (not all of them spent at university) before I produced another and started to regularly achieve high marks. So what changed? Two things. First, I became interested in what I was studying. Second, I came to understand the purpose of university essays. This is what I realised: there is nothing mysterious about a university essay. Typically, it provides an answer to a question (a solution to a problem) following a considered exploration of a subject. 'Considered exploration' means that relevant perspectives are introduced and analysed in a systematic manner. While the answer is important – we ask questions because we want answers – it is the considered exploration which scores most of the marks. This is because an answer has little value if it is not obtained through a sound process.

The essay continues to exist because it is a flexible form that is well suited to exploring complex problems that often cannot be solved using empirical methods (that is, by conducting studies, experiments and so on). The important point is that such problems exist everywhere, not just in academia. They include who to vote for in an election, what to do about climate change and even how to be a good parent. Thus, if you become skilled at being able to identify the key issues in relation to a particular problem, weighing the reasoning and evidence advanced in support of different perspectives, and ultimately making your own informed arguments, you will not just be a good essay writer, you will have acquired broad life skills.

What to expect from this book

There are two approaches to teaching essay writing; the approaches overlap and are often taught together. The first is to teach the process of essay writing, namely the stages a student ought to move through to craft a good essay. The second is to identify the characteristics of a good essay. As there are already some excellent books that give detailed instructions about how to craft a good essay, such as Greetham's *How To Write Better Essays* (2013), this book focuses on providing a clearly structured, comprehensive account of the characteristics of a good essay. Having said this, advice about the essay writing process will appear periodically.

How to use this book

You do not need to read this book from beginning to end. The book is structured around the key areas of essay assessment, and each chapter can be read on its own. You might, for instance, like to begin by exploring one of the chapters on structure from later in the book (Chapters 7–11), and only later return, say, to Chapter 2 on critical thinking. The following is an overview of what will appear in each chapter.

- Chapter 1 ('Essay writing in the university context, marking criteria and markers') explains how essay writing relates to the broader purpose of universities and clarifies the specific criteria that will be used to mark your essays.
- Chapter 2 ('Critical thinking') introduces the foundational concept, 'critical thinking'. The chapter is located early in the book because critical thinking is present in almost all aspects of essay writing. Thirteen key characteristics of critical thinking are outlined.
- Chapter 3 ('Engaging with others' work: the fundamentals') and Chapter 4 ('How others' work can help you develop your arguments') explain how to incorporate others' work into your essays. The former covers the mechanics of incorporating others' work and the latter explains the different ways that others' work can feature in your arguments.
- Chapter 5 ('Academic writing style, grammar and layout') provides advice about how to write in an academic manner. There is also advice about grammar and how to present your essays.
- Chapter 6 ('The essay question') tells you what you need to keep in mind when selecting, analysing and responding to essay questions.
- Chapters 7–11 ('Structure and signposting', 'Essay introductions', 'Rules for writing body paragraphs', 'Different body paragraph structures' and 'Essay conclusions') all deal with how to structure an essay. Chapter 7 is

concerned with the general structure of essays and the subsequent chapters with the structures of the different components of essays: introductions, body paragraphs and conclusions.

- Chapter 12 ('Analysing complete essays') consolidates all that has been covered in the book by 'marking' two complete essays. You will also have the opportunity to put yourself in the marker's shoes and mark an essay.

Throughout the book the advice given is illustrated with examples drawn from a wide range of student essays and occasionally from academic publications. Not only will these examples help you understand the advice, you will be able to draw on the language and structures used when writing your own essays. Each chapter also contains activities so you can practise the skills that have been covered. Answers, where relevant, are at the back of the book. Sometimes the material in different chapters overlaps. This has been allowed to ensure not only that each topic is exhaustively dealt with, but so that you can see the interconnected nature of the different aspects of essay writing. At times you will be directed to related discussions in different chapters.

Who this book is for

This book has been written primarily for undergraduate and taught (coursework) postgraduate students whose assessments will include essays. I have tried to ensure that the book is inclusive of all disciplines by using a wide variety of examples and by sometimes pointing out the different ways that disciplines approach essay writing.

However, even though the book is about essay writing, much of the advice given will be relevant to other forms of academic writing, in that many assignment forms require well-crafted paragraphs, appropriately integrated sources and so on. Students producing dissertations will find this book particularly useful given the similarities between essays and dissertations. Academics can also benefit from it when setting assignments.

Some words of encouragement and warning

If you follow the advice in this book your essay writing will improve rapidly. However, you should always keep in mind that essay writing – indeed all writing – is an art. This means that for every essay you produce, you will need to use your own ingenuity to solve many of the problems you encounter. Therefore, among other things, believe in yourself and take some risks. Also, there will be situations when the advice given can, and perhaps should, be ignored. Not only do rules sometimes need to be broken, but different disciplines, universities and countries have different ways of writing. Although, when such situations arise, you should recall why the advice was given and be able to explain – at least to yourself – why you should do something different.

Understanding the Purpose of University Essays

Introduction

Writing a good essay involves providing an answer to a given question, or, once again, a solution to a problem. However, there is much more to it than that. You also need to demonstrate that you have a number of characteristics. These characteristics are closely related to the broader purpose of universities themselves and can be identified in most marking criteria. By exploring the broader purpose of universities and providing an overview of the criteria that will be used to mark your essays, this chapter will equip you with the 'first principles' of essay writing. Once you understand these, much of the time you will be able to work out yourself what you need to do to score well in a given essay. The chapter will finish by saying a few words about the people who will be marking your essays.

> **Develop your own criteria** ACTIVITY 1.1
>
> Before you read on, come up with a set of criteria that you think could be used to mark an essay. Justify why you have selected each criterion. Compare your criteria with Box 1.2 on page 4.

Understanding essays in the university context

A glance across various university 'mission statements', 'visions' and 'strategic plans' reveals a clear common purpose for all universities: to create and disseminate knowledge. Knowledge is created through research and is disseminated through publication and teaching.

When talking about creating knowledge, universities use a range of related words. Some will speak about being 'innovative', or say they foster 'independence'. Some emphasise that their researchers focus on 'critical issues'. But regardless of the word choice, the goal is the same. Interestingly, it is regularly stated that the work carried out at universities benefits the world, that is, creating knowledge is seen as a progressive, moral act.

With respect to disseminating knowledge, universities provide knowledge about specific subjects as well as vocational training.

Importantly, universities also say that they inculcate in their students an *intellectual discipline* which is broadly useful. This discipline, which is often referred to as critical thinking, is a core aspect of knowledge creation, and is also valuable when we perform everyday tasks such as deciding on a course of action or assessing whether a piece of information is believable.

To summarise, the purpose of universities is to create and disseminate knowledge for the benefit of the world, and to develop individual capabilities that are both subject-specific and transferrable.

What does all of this have to do with essays?

As a student you have a mixed identity. In part it is your job to gain knowledge about and learn the skills specific to your discipline. However, you also need to start behaving like a creator of knowledge. This second part of your identity should become more pronounced as you progress (do not worry, you have time!). But how, no doubt you are wondering, is this manifest in essay writing? Box 1.1 contains the core characteristics of a creator of knowledge; these are the characteristics you need to demonstrate in your essays. Attend closely to them. We will return to them throughout this book.

Box 1.1   The core characteristics of a creator of knowledge

A creator of knowledge:
1. has knowledge about their subject
2. understands the complexities within their subject (including key problems and debates, the subject's history and gaps in the body of knowledge)
3. is able to evaluate the various positions within their subject and clearly present their own original perspectives

---

Again, there is nothing mysterious about this. A creator of knowledge has knowledge and is able to think critically about this knowledge and build upon it, all in a manner that can be understood by others. This is similar to being, say, a fan of tennis or football: you know the rules of the game, player profiles, statistics, and so on; you understand the various debates and controversies that exist; and you have lots of opinions about how the game should be played and run.

Marking criteria

The criteria that will be used to assess your essays follow naturally from the core characteristics of a creator of knowledge. Box 1.2 identifies the broad assessment criteria that will be used and details the desirable and undesirable characteristics within each criterion. Multiple marking criteria from different universities were consulted. But do not be overwhelmed! The desirable characteristics are there to give you a sense of what you need to work towards to achieve the highest marks, not what you have to do to pass your next essay. The broad criteria are listed in roughly the same order as they appear in the later chapters.

When looking at generic marking criteria from your university or marking criteria for specific courses, be aware that even though the wording and organisation can vary considerably, *what is generally required rarely changes*. Wording and organisation vary because assessment criteria overlap heavily, meaning there is no obvious objective way to structure the information.

Different types of essays: the research essay, the reflective essay and the exam essay

The main type of essay you will have to write is the 'research' essay. For this you will be given a question and have anywhere from a few days to a few months to research and write. This book is focused on teaching you how to write this kind of essay. However, you may also encounter 'reflective' essays or have to write essays in exam situations. These do not require a major change in technique, but rather a shift in focus; this shift should be made clear in the guidelines for the task. While I will not go into detail about these subgenres of essay writing, a few points can be made.

Reflective essays, as the name suggests, usually encourage you to express what you think. They are often designed to encourage critical thinking rather than your ability to engage in a detailed manner with the relevant literature. However, what is required can vary considerably.

Exam essays present different challenges. These include the fact that they will usually be shorter than research essays, so you have to get to the point quickly, and, in the case of closed book exams, you will not have access to sources. Often success in exam essays can be achieved simply by demonstrating knowledge; although, as noted in the course guide for the Philosophy course, 'Morality & Value' at the University of Edinburgh, 'part of the exercise will be for the student to work out the extent to which the question calls for something going beyond pure exegesis'. In other words, a successful essay may need to explore the complexities of the subject and

Box 1.2   Desirable and undesirable characteristics of essays

Broad criteria	Desirable	Undesirable
Knowledge and understanding (Chapters 2–4)	• Command of the literature is either broad or detailed • Knowledge and understanding is demonstrated of key works and relevant facts, problems, debates, theories and concepts • Awareness is demonstrated of the complexities of the issues • Reading goes beyond what is required • Sources are peer reviewed and come from respected journals and publishers	• Sources are limited, dated, irrelevant or non-peer reviewed • No awareness is shown of key works, relevant problems, and so on • There is a heavy reliance on a handful of sources • Others' views are inaccurately presented
Critical thinking (Chapter 2)	• Strong reasoning and evidence are used to support arguments • There is clarity of 'voice' • Independent or bold analysis is undertaken • Obvious objections are anticipated • Assumptions of others are identified and tested	• Claims are not supported with reasoning or evidence • Analysis is poor or absent • Arguments and evidence are taken at face value • Engagement with sources is unimaginative
Use and integration of sources and referencing (Chapters 3 & 4)	• Use includes analysis, comparison and contrast, evaluation and synthesis • Strong illustrations are used • Referencing is accurate	• A simple factual approach is taken • Referencing is inconsistent/does not follow guidelines

Grammar, expression and layout (Chapter 5)	• Writing is distinguished by sophistication, nuance and regard for style • Style is fluent and engaging • Grammar and spelling are flawless • Presentation guidelines are followed	• Response is not able to be understood • There are multiple grammatical and spelling errors • Style is informal
Answering the question (Chapter 6)	• Question is clearly and coherently answered • Response remains focused on the question throughout • Naïve aspects of the question are challenged	• Question is not addressed • Large amounts of irrelevant material are included
Structure (Chapters 7–11)	• Structure provides a sound basis for addressing the question • A thesis is present when appropriate • Argument (thesis) is sustained throughout the essay • Argument is logical • Purpose of each part is indicated • Relationship between parts is clear • Conclusion is justified by the evidence	• There is little or no evidence of structure • Essay regularly strays from the point or loses focus

Sources consulted: Department of Life Sciences, Imperial College London; Department of Psychology, Macquarie University; Faculty of Law, University of Auckland; Faculty of Modern and Medieval Languages, University of Cambridge; King's College London; Research School of Management, Australian National University; School of English, University of Sussex; School of Modern Languages, University of Bristol; School of Philosophy, Psychology and Language Sciences, University of Edinburgh; School of Social Sciences, University of New South Wales; University of Exeter; University of Liverpool.

present an original perspective. Exam essays should still include the usual structural elements, and while you might need to refer to others' work, rigorous referencing is often not required.

Who your marker is and why thinking about this matters

Some of your markers will be professors and others will be completing their doctoral degrees. Some will be magnanimous and others pedantic. Some will dedicate considerable time to reviewing your work and others, often because of pressures not of their own making, will review your work quickly. When producing your essays it is important to take the worst-case scenario into account; while a magnanimous professor with lots of time on her hands may be inclined to look somewhat kindly upon a chaotic, under-researched, poorly edited essay which nonetheless contains moments of genius, a pedantic postgraduate student who has to mark 100 essays in a week and who is only being paid to spend 12 minutes per essay, despite the fact that it takes 30 minutes to do a good job, may not.

The point is that you want to keep your marker in 'happy mode', not push them into 'annoyed mode'. While an annoyed marker will try to be fair-minded, clearly you are better off with a happy marker. This is particularly important when your mark sits at the threshold between marking bands. The happy marker will be more likely to push your mark into the higher band than the annoyed marker.

What will make a marker happy or annoyed? Read the rest of this book and you will find out, of course! However, below are three things most essay writers should be able to achieve.

- Avoid making common errors in your expression and grammar and have a good layout (for example, decent line spacing and margins). Sloppy writing and layout makes the marker think that you do not care about your work. They then think, if the student does not care, then why should I care? See Chapter 5.
- Ensure that your referencing follows the appropriate conventions. Sloppy referencing immediately makes the marker sense laziness, or worse, plagiarism. Referencing guidelines are easily obtained.
- Ensure that your essay has a clear skeleton. In a typical essay this means including a succinct thesis or general answer to the question in your introduction, and ensuring that each of your paragraphs begins with a clear topic sentence which indicates how the paragraph contributes to your argument and ultimately helps to answer the question. Even if your

argument is not as well research or nuanced as it might be, at least your marker will not struggle to work out what you are saying. See Chapter 7.

Conclusion

This chapter has clarified what, generally speaking, you need to do to achieve high marks in your essays. The main point to take away is that usually it is not enough to reproduce the ideas of others; you need to do something with these ideas. This is because as a university student you need to begin to behave like a creator of knowledge. Remember, a creator of knowledge is able to:

- demonstrate knowledge about their subject
- explore the complexities within their subject
- clearly present their own original perspectives

We have also seen the broad criteria that will be used to mark your essays and begun to explore the desirable and undesirable characteristics within each of these. The remainder of this book will examine all of these characteristics in detail. Finally, you have been encouraged to think about your marker whenever you write. Do whatever you can to keep them happy!

Critical Thinking

Introduction

Critical thinking is essential not only for producing strong university essays but for any activity that calls for information to be evaluated and for problems to be solved (for knowledge to be created). While there are many facets to critical thinking, in a nutshell it involves two things:

- questioning claims about the nature of the world and about what people ought to do, and,
- if any claim is found not to be supported by sound reasoning and evidence, devising a better claim.

Those who do not think critically tend to accept the ideas of others without sufficiently questioning them, or else they make their own claims but their reasoning and evidence are weak.

Echoing what was said in the previous chapter, for most of your essays, to do well you will need to explore what various people say in relation to a subject and whenever possible you should include your own considered perspectives.

This chapter will expand on these points by reviewing 13 characteristics of critical thinking. As mentioned, the chapter appears early in this book because critical thinking underpins most of the skills needed to produce high-quality essays; many of the discussions here will be taken up again later. Given the chapter's more general nature, it can be skipped if you would like to focus on specific aspects of essay writing. Keep in mind that while you will be able to improve the structure of your introductions, paragraphs and conclusions straight away by following the advice in this book, it will probably take some time before you will be able to confidently display the 13 characteristics of critical thinking. To give you some help, the chapter finishes by providing some advice about how to improve your critical thinking.

Being knowledgeable

If you know little about a subject it will be difficult to discuss it in a meaningful way, and it will be almost impossible to make original contributions. So, the first characteristic of critical thinking is *knowing* what is generally accepted in a subject.

Keep in mind that at university the onus is on you to educate yourself. Lectures, textbooks and set readings are only a starting point. To appear genuinely knowledgeable you will need to locate your own sources and find ways to incorporate them in your essays. Chapters 3 and 4 will provide you with lots of advice about the mechanics of incorporating others' work into your essays as well as about some of the more sophisticated things you can do with others' work.

Having understanding

However, having knowledge is just the first step. If you do not do anything with it, you will not score highly. As the Faculty of Law at the University of Auckland states, assignments around the fail/pass threshold 'take a simple factual approach'.

While in many subjects there will be a pool of largely uncontested facts, there will also be a great many claims that are still being contested. Much of the work carried out in universities takes place in this zone of contestation. Thus, for every claim made within a subject, the strongest critical thinkers will be able to say something about the extent to which the claim is established as fact. This will involve not only evaluating the reasoning and evidence used to support the claim, but knowing how the claim relates to other claims in the subject and accounting for differences. In the words of the University of Exeter, the best work is able to 'investigate contradictory information and identify reasons for contradictions'. The School of Modern Languages at the University of Bristol makes a similar point when it states that assignments in the top two bands 'deal with complexity, contradictions or gaps in the knowledge base'.

But do not worry too much if you are not yet able to demonstrate this kind of understanding. It takes time. Sometimes a year or two, usually more. However, if you want to start down the path of understanding, whenever you are reading and writing, think about how you can *compare*, *contrast*, *evaluate* and *synthesise* (combine) different perspectives (see Chapter 4).

Demonstrating understanding by exploring complexity

Below are three uncritical (black and white) statements. Pick one and come up with as many points as you can which both support and refute the statement. By doing this you will be exploring the complexities of the subject.

Statements
1 The internet is good
2 The world is becoming a better place
3 Gender equality has been achieved

Being sceptical

As mentioned, critical thinking involves not accepting that a claim about the world is true simply because someone, even an expert, says it is. All claims must be evaluated.

Importantly, in your essays you should evaluate not just what other people say, but what you yourself say. The strongest essays not only present careful reasoning and good evidence to support their claims, they anticipate objections to these claims, present these objections and in good faith explain why they should not be accepted. This point is made in marking criteria for a Philosophy course at the University of Edinburgh. We read, 'The author considers the most important objections to his/her arguments/views. The replies are generally convincing and subtle.' If you do find that the objections you anticipate should be accepted, then you must change your position! You will see some good examples of anticipating objections in the second sample essay in Chapter 12.

Those who are new to university can find being sceptical challenging. This is because in secondary school the emphasis is on gaining and demonstrating knowledge rather than questioning and creating new knowledge.

Recognising and working with patterns

One of the main aspects of critical thinking is recognising and working with patterns. By 'patterns' I mean regularities in phenomena, for instance, the orbits of planets, the effect of a type of therapy or similarities between the arguments of different authors. To clarify, imagine that two people read two novels which tell very different stories but contain similar themes. The uncritical person notices that the plots and settings are different and believes that because of this the books are different. The critical person sees the thematic similarities beneath the different plots and settings and believes that the books are not as different as they might first appear.

Importantly, when we speak about knowledge, often we are speaking about *knowledge of patterns*. Similarly, a theory, a thesis (the general argument made in an essay) and even individual points within paragraphs, are often accounts of patterns. For example, Adam Smith's theory of 'the invisible hand which guides us' putatively identifies the pattern that if individuals pursue their own interests, this will indirectly benefit society. And, if I make the general argument in an essay that the world is, for the most part, becoming a better place, I am identifying a general pattern of improvement.

Being able to recognise and work with patterns makes us versatile. On this point, in marking criteria from the Department of Philosophy at the University of York it is stated that the best students will be able to '[a]pply ideas learned in one situation to new situations'. Clearly, being able to do this is an asset for solving problems both inside and outside university.

Identifying patterns	ACTIVITY 2.2

A question regularly encountered at university is, 'What is human nature?' Most disciplines tackle this question in one way or another. Either on your own or as part of a group consider the following related question: are there *patterns* in human behaviour that allow us to know some aspects of human nature (that allow us to differentiate between 'nature' and 'nurture')?

Making logical arguments (using reasoning)

Critical thinking involves making logical arguments. When an argument is logical it follows certain principles of reasoning. To explore these principles in any detail is beyond the scope of this book; however, even if you are not able to identify different logical forms (few can unless they have taken a course in logic or read a book about it), you will nonetheless have an intuitive sense of what logic is and will be able to spot when an argument is illogical. To demonstrate, let us consider the following argument. 'Samia plays ultimate frisbee. Samia is great. Therefore all ultimate frisbee players are great.' Even if you do not know what a syllogism is, you can see that something is wrong with this argument. No doubt you are thinking something like, 'The fact that Samia plays ultimate frisbee and is great has very little bearing on whether other ultimate frisbee players are great.' A logical argument would be, 'Samia plays ultimate frisbee. All ultimate frisbee players are great. Therefore Samia is great.' Clearly in this instance, if Samia plays ultimate frisbee there is no option but for her to be great.

Example 2.1, which is drawn from a student's essay, contains some flawed logic. The essay was responding to the question, 'Is there a difference between good and bad science fiction?'

Example 2.1   Flawed logic

Essay question
Is there a difference between good and bad science fiction?

The first three sentences from the essay
[1] There is no definitive definition of science fiction (SF), only broad or narrow interpretations of what constitutes SF (Freedman 2000, p.13). [2] Different definitions of science fiction give rise to different expectations of what constitutes good science fiction. [3] Hence, it can be argued that good science fiction is defined by how much the reader or audience accepts a work's novum, where a novum is understood as the central scientific innovation of a work (see Suvin 1979).

Analysis
The first two sentences give the impression that the essay will go on to outline several criteria – perhaps even conflicting criteria – for differentiating between good and bad science fiction. Instead, in the third sentence, the student provides one overarching criterion. This is illogical.

Is the student's approach logical?   ACTIVITY 2.3

See if you can identify a flaw in the student's logic. Compare what the student argues in their thesis (their general argument) with the third and final point from the outline of the essay. Both the thesis and the outline come from the essay's introduction.

Essay question
Artificial intelligence is often considered to be a threat to humanity. Is this concern justified?

Essay's thesis
This essay will argue that artificial intelligence will only become a threat to humanity if it reaches sovereign consciousness. Sovereign consciousness involves having self-ownership over consciousness, that is, having autonomy over mind and body.

Third point from the essay's outline
Finally, it will be argued that self-governing artificial intelligence will threaten the safety of humanity if it is not programmed with the core goal of philanthropy.

Using evidence

Using evidence goes hand in hand with recognising patterns and using reasoning, and when the three are artfully combined, critical thinking is well demonstrated. In more detail, whenever we make any claim about the existence of a pattern we need to substantiate this with evidence; however, reasoning often must be used to ensure that the evidence is convincing. Example 2.2 shows how evidence can be combined with reasoning to substantiate a claim about a pattern. The example involves a discussion of the phenomenon of 'price bubbles'.

Example 2.2   Evidence combined with reasoning to substantiate a claim about a pattern

Consider the claim that there is a pattern that people are often unable to recognise a price bubble when they are in the middle of one. (A price bubble occurs when the price of something, for example, housing, rapidly increases to a level substantially above its true value. This is often the consequence of a strong demand which is driven by the search for quick profits. A bubble is followed by a rapid deflation of prices – the bubble bursts.) We could support this claim by conducting a long-term study of people's opinions about whether they are in the middle of a bubble and determining the extent to which these opinions correlate with actual bubbles. However, this would take decades to do well. A different approach, very much suited to essay writing, would be to find what experts themselves have said just before price bubbles burst. Our reasoning for doing this would be that if highly trained and experienced people were unable to detect bubbles, then the average person will also struggle. We could then quote US Secretary of the Treasury, Andrew Mellon, who, in September 1929 said, 'There is no cause to worry. The high tide of prosperity will continue', and US Federal Reserve chief Alan Greenspan, who, in June 2005 said, 'Although we certainly cannot rule out home price declines, especially in some local markets, these declines, were they to occur, likely would not have substantial macroeconomic implications.' Both of these remarks were made shortly before price bubbles burst.

Note that we use evidence not just to substantiate claims about patterns, but also to substantiate claims about the existence and causes of events. For example, if we want to substantiate the claim that a historical figure was the father of a certain child, we could, say, present a letter he wrote to the child's mother in which he discusses his parental responsibilities.

A question frequently asked by students is, 'When can a claim be substantiated by referring to common knowledge, and when does research need to be cited?' There is no simple answer to this question. Ultimately, the more you become familiar with a subject and, more generally, with critical thinking, the more you will get a sense of what counts as 'common knowledge' within a subject and what does not. Example 2.3 presents an argument which largely draws on common knowledge, specifically, our common knowledge of mass shootings and the rule of law.

Example 2.3   An argument which largely draws on common knowledge

A prominent Australian political cartoonist, Michael Leunig, has drawn some controversial cartoons which support parents who do not vaccinate their children because of fears that vaccination might harm their children. One reason Leunig gives for his position is that he admires the person who stands alone: the person who resists the will of the majority. We can respond by arguing that even though the person who stands alone against a corrupt majority is an attractive and enduring trope – such people appear again and again in history, books and movies, for example, Katniss Everdeen in *The Hunger Games* – we can also point to many examples of people who stand alone for questionable reasons and who perform questionable acts. Those responsible for mass shootings are a good example. We can also point out that numerous good things exist which are supported by the majority, such as the rule of law, which exists precisely to dissuade individuals from acting rashly or corruptly because of their idiosyncratic beliefs. The general point is that the person who stands alone ought not to be admired simply because they stand alone; their beliefs and actions must be evaluated in context. Thus, Leunig's argument should not be accepted.

Being systematic

A critical thinker wants to communicate their ideas with the world; therefore, it is important for them to develop their arguments systematically. When we are systematic we make use of some kind of organisational logic. For example, if we are considering whether something should be done, it would be systematic first to consider all the reasons why it should be done, and then all the reasons why it should not be done. An unsystematic approach would be to consider reasons for and against in a haphazard manner. The more haphazard an argument is, the harder it is to follow. There are a number of conventions for how to produce a systematic essay, many of which will be covered in Chapters 7–11.

Being efficient

Being efficient means expressing yourself using the fewest words possible. The relevance for critical thinking is once again that a critical thinker tries to communicate clearly. It is all too easy in intellectual work to allow our arguments and even sentences to become wordy and overly complex. This can occur when we are seduced by trying to sound intelligent rather than trying to reveal the truth as we see it (see the discussion of technical terms on p. 48), but it can also be a simple matter of sloppy writing (see the discussion of wordiness on p. 51). This advice must be balanced against the problem of oversimplifying complex phenomena.

Being consistent

The need for consistency is present in many aspects of writing.

- You should maintain structural consistency. For example, if three points are introduced in the order A, B, C, you should not discuss them in the order B, C, A.
- You should be consistent in your use of words. For example, if you say that you will refer to 'science fiction' as 'SF', you should not then write 'sci fi' (see the discussion of consistent word use on p. 53).
- Your arguments should be logically consistent. On this point, the Faculty of Law at the University of Auckland states that essays which fail, 'may state contradictory propositions'.
- The principles/assumptions that underpin your arguments should be consistent. This is more challenging because these are not always expressed. For example, at one point an argument might contain the assumption that individuals are responsible for their actions, whereas at another point an argument might assume that social forces determine individuals' actions, reducing their responsibility.

Being flexible

Being flexible is a key aspect of critical thinking because a critical thinker believes what they believe because of reasoning and evidence. When existing reasoning and evidence are shown to be wrong, a critical thinker changes their beliefs. This attitude is reflected in the following remark by the economist, John Maynard Keynes: 'When my information changes, I alter my conclusions. What do you do, sir?' Flexibility can be demonstrated by being cautious when drawing conclusions from imperfect evidence (see p. 48).

Being independent

Being independent is implied in several of the above points. While a critical thinker will frequently consult others, ultimately the work they produce will be the product of their own will and intellectual processes. The School of Modern Languages at the University of Bristol makes this point when it states that the best assignments display 'creativity, originality, [and] autonomy'. Thinking about the marking experience, when reading the work of a strong critical thinker, a marker will have the impression that the student can be trusted to identify and solve important problems on their own. This is the best impression to create, not just with markers but with employers!

There are many ways to display independence. For example, you can find your own good-quality sources, that is, not just rely on the sources recommended by your teachers. You can also make thoughtful critiques and nuanced arguments. However, more simply, independence can be displayed by ensuring your voice is present in a number of key places in your essays. Box 2.1 outlines some of these places. Note that there is a close relationship between this advice and the advice about signposting in Chapter 7. This is because signposting is one of the main ways to make your voice heard. See Example 3.1 in the next chapter for an instance of a paragraph with no voice.

Being self-aware

A critical thinker is self-aware. In their writing they give the impression that they regularly turn their critical eye towards their own thoughts and work. A strong way to give an impression of self-awareness is to justify the decisions that you make in your writing: a good writer does not just say *what* they will do but *why* they are doing it. You can do this in your introduction, but you can also do this as you introduce new points in the body of your essay. For example, 'Having considered X, we now need to examine Y for of reason Z.' We also sense self-awareness when objections to arguments are anticipated and dealt with.

Being principled

The claim that a critical thinker is principled is contentious; however, it is unavoidable. The most important principle a critical thinker should embrace is that truths exist and they matter. Truths exist because, as

> ### Box 2.1   Places you can make your voice heard
>
> You can make your voice heard in the following places.
>
> - When, in your introduction, you introduce your subject and the question/problem you are addressing and explain why the subject/question/problem is significant (see p. 89).
> - When, in your introduction, you present your general argument (thesis) in response to the essay question (not all essays will introduce a general argument in the introduction; see p. 95).
> - When you use the first sentence or two in each body paragraph to clarify how your argument is developing and to introduce the specific point to be addressed in the paragraph (see p. 108).
> - When, at the end of a body paragraph, you clarify how a point you are making supports your general argument and ultimately helps you to answer the question (see p. 112).
> - When you use transition signals such as 'however', 'furthermore' and 'specifically' to make it clear how different sentences relate to one another (see p. 110).
> - When you use reporting verbs and phrases such as 'Wang argues that ...' to integrate others' work into your essay. When you are doing this you are differentiating between your voice and others' voices (see p. 30).
> - When you analyse others' work (see Chapter 4).
> - When you show caution when making a claim (see p. 48).
> - When, in your conclusion, you clarify how the arguments you have made in the body support your general response to the question (see Chapter 11).

discussed earlier, patterns exist: patterns in the physical world and in the actions and thoughts of people. Truths also exist for the even simpler reason that things happen; the idea being that once something has happened, it becomes a historical truth. Truths matter because if we are able to understand the nature of the world – the patterns within it and what has happened – then we will be able to manipulate the world to improve lives, including our own, and even the well-being of humanity and the planet as a whole. This belief in the possibility of progress is, as mentioned in the previous chapter, a guiding principle of many universities.

Often in conflict with the pursuit of truth – though not necessarily so – is the pursuit of power, success and belonging. For some, each of these last three can become an end such that the truth is sacrificed. This happens when someone plagiarises or overuses fashionable jargon to entrench themselves in an intellectual community. The truth is also sacrificed when we twist evidence to suit our needs. You may be familiar with the saying, 'lies, damn lies and statistics'. This saying implies that statistics can be used to justify anything because they are easy to misrepresent. However, we can thank the *principled* use of statistics for many of the things we enjoy in the world today.

Thinking critically about critical thinking   ACTIVITY 2.4

Hopefully you are already employing your critical faculties and are interrogating the above characteristics of critical thinking. Are you convinced? The following are some challenging questions you might like to consider. Some thoughts in relation to questions 4, 5 and 6 are provided in the Appendix.

1 Can you think of an aspect of critical thinking that is missing or that did not receive sufficient attention?
2 Can what is missing be incorporated into one of the given characteristics?
3 Can you think of a more efficient way of expressing the characteristics?
4 What do you think about the final point that critical thinking involves being principled? Why might this be controversial?
5 When has critical thinking improved the world?
6 When has critical thinking damaged the world and what does this say about critical thinking?

But what can I do to think critically?

In the previous chapter I pointed out that there is little difference between being a creator of knowledge and being, say, a tennis or football fan. As mentioned, both a creator of knowledge and a sports fan have knowledge about their subject, are able to think critically about this knowledge and also build upon it. I mention this again to make the point that almost everyone thinks critically in some aspect of their lives, whether it be in their appreciation of sport, in their pursuit of a hobby or even in how they manage relationships. The difficulty for many students is activating their critical thinking faculties in the university context. What you need to do to think critically at university is straightforward. The challenge is having the will power to do it. Below I list four related things you can do to improve your critical thinking.

- Take an interest in what you study (or study what you are interested in).
- Do (parts of) your course readings and go to class.

- Find and read good-quality sources and make good notes from them.
- Start working early.

Let us consider these in a more detail.

Take an interest

A useful bit of wisdom is that teachers do not actually teach students. Students teach themselves. The point is that no matter how brilliant your teacher is, if you are not interested in a subject you will not focus your attention on it, and thus you will struggle to learn the relevant information, you will not feel inclined to understand the subject's complexities and you will not form your own opinions.

One of the great benefits of interest is that you will think about your subject more often and maybe even look things up in your spare time, just because you are curious. This casual repetition and exploration is one of the keys to thinking critically.

Do (parts of) your readings and go to class

Following closely from the previous point, if you want to think critically about a subject, do your course readings. But do not become a reading martyr! Do not make yourself read all your readings from beginning to end, thinking that just because the words have passed through your brain you will have got something out of them. You are sometimes better off carefully reading the first couple of pages of a source and perhaps also the conclusion, and being clear about the problem being addressed (including the broader context of the problem), the proposed solution and how the reading relates to the course and especially to the essay you will write. If you combine doing this with going to class, paying attention and getting involved in discussions, you will be exposing your brain multiple times each week to key information, problems, debates and so on. When the time comes to write your essay, you will already have a strong *understanding* of your subject.

Find quality sources and make good notes from them

When preparing for your essays you need to find good-quality sources (more is said about the quality of sources in Chapter 3, see p. 24). Once you have found these sources you need to make good notes from them. Good notes have two main characteristics:

- They only include information that is relevant for the course and especially for the essay you are preparing for. Students are mistaken in thinking that making good notes merely involves summarising a source. This approach is too passive. A critical thinker is always asking, 'How can this source help me?'

- They include the thoughts you have about what you are reading. These thoughts are your own critical voice, and once again, they should be responding to the question, 'How can this source help me?' Record whether you think a point is good or bad. Record similarities and differences between different sources. Record how a point from the source might feature in your essay. From these recorded thoughts your essay will grow. (See Chapter 4 for a detailed discussion of how others' work can help you develop your arguments.)

Start working early

It is rarely true that intelligent people produce great work at the last minute. Every now and then a couple of days of feverish, inspired labour can produce surprising results, but usually good work takes time. More than anything you need time to write, put aside what you have written and come back to your writing with fresh eyes. The more you can do this the more sophisticated and precise your writing will become.

Conclusion

Drawing together all that has been said, critical thinking is manifest in three general ways.

- It involves *having a sophisticated kind of knowledge*, that is, not just knowing facts but understanding the complexities of a subject and being able to recognise patterns.
- It involves *having certain attitudes*. These include being sceptical, flexible, independent, self-aware and principled.
- It involves *presenting your ideas in a certain way*. You should support your claims with reasoning and evidence, and your arguments should be expressed systematically and efficiently.

We shall return to all these points throughout this book.

Chapter 3

Engaging with Others' Work: The Fundamentals

Introduction

As has been discussed, including others' work in your essays allows you to do a number of important things. It helps you to demonstrate that you are knowledgeable about your subject and it provides you with a context within which you can create new knowledge. Also, analysing others' work is a good way to demonstrate critical thinking. Finally – and perhaps most obviously – by drawing on others' work you can strengthen your own arguments. However, to do any of these things successfully (see Chapter 4 for details), you must have the basic skills to differentiate between your voice and the voices of others, that is, between your words and ideas and others' words and ideas. This chapter will introduce these skills. It will begin with a brief discussion of plagiarism before considering the quality of different sources of information and explaining how exactly to integrate others' work into your essays.

Plagiarism

This discussion of plagiarism will be brief because all universities have well-developed and easily accessed information about plagiarism. The focus will be the aspects of plagiarism that are most relevant to honest students. On this point, it is important to remember that plagiarism is not a uniform category; rather, it is a spectrum. It ranges from copying large tracts of others' work without acknowledgement to using too many paraphrases.

Forms of plagiarism relevant to honest students

Quoting without quotation marks or acknowledgement

If you are inexperienced with tertiary studies, you may not realise that when you use the exact words of someone else, these words must appear between quotation marks and the source of the quotation must be appropriately acknowledged.

Paraphrasing or summarising without acknowledgement

Paraphrasing or summarising involves expressing others' ideas in your own words. As these ideas are not your own, the original source must be acknowledged, regardless of how different the wording is.

Too much paraphrasing (the 'plagiphrase')

Even if you acknowledge all your sources you can still be guilty of plagiarism if your own voice is insufficiently present. This type of plagiarism is jokingly referred to as 'plagiphrasing' and often occurs in work produced by students who are struggling to understand their subject. To 'survive' their essays, these students build their essays by joining together fully acknowledged paraphrases of others' work.

Example 3.1 presents a plagiphrase. The example is the first body paragraph from an International Relations essay responding to the question, 'What is humanitarian intervention? Should humanitarian interventions occur?'

Example 3.1   The plagiphrase

Essay question
What is humanitarian intervention? Should humanitarian interventions occur?

First paragraph of the body of the essay
Humanitarian intervention is a coercive act by an external party aimed to prevent or alleviate a mass humanitarian violation within the territorial jurisdiction of a state in the absence of local governmental consent (Macklem 2008). The legal status of humanitarian intervention is contested. For the most part, intervention violates interpretations of customary as well as codified international law (Buchanan 1999). In contrast to earlier eras, there has evolved a general presumption against the use of force (Ramsbotham 1997). The central contemporary debate is concerned with the binary nature of jurisdiction identified in the UN Charter between 'state system values' and 'human rights values' (Macklem 2008, p. 369).

Analysis
While the information presented is of a high quality and relevant, the student's voice is absent. None of the markers of 'voice' that were introduced in the previous chapter (see Box 2.1) can be identified: the paragraph lacks a topic sentence in the student's own words, the paraphrases are not introduced, the student does not indicate how the sentences are related, there is no analysis of the material, and the student does not mention how the material helps to answer the question.

But how could this paragraph have been written differently? One approach is that the student could have made greater use of summaries. Summaries can be useful because, as will be discussed below, they demonstrate a broad knowledge of a subject and also the student's ability to combine (or synthesise) information from different sources. Example 3.2 is a template of how the paragraph in Example 3.1 could have been better approached (it is not a simple rewrite).

Inaccurate referencing

As has been stated, all words and ideas produced by someone else which are included in your assignments must be referenced. Correct referencing

---

Example 3.2   An improvement on the plagiphrase

The first paragraph and the beginning of the second of the body of the essay
[1] There is some debate about the nature of humanitarian intervention (HI). [2] Most (see for example X; Y; Z) believe that humanitarian interventions require some form of military force; [3] whereas some (see A; B) broaden the definition to include non-military actions such as sanctions and providing aid. [4] Both perspectives will be explored in detail before a preferred definition is given.

[5] The core elements of HI involving military force are as follows.

Analysis
- [1]–[4] This brief paragraph functions as a mini introduction for the first section of the essay which will explore definitions of HI.
- [1] This first sentence is in the student's own words. The use of 'some' indicates a nuanced understanding of the topic; specifically, that while debate exists, there is a reasonably strong consensus.
- [2] The words 'Most believe' indicate that a summary of others' perspectives is about to be presented. Also, 'Most believe', when combined with mentioning researchers X, Y and Z, generates the impression that the student has a broad knowledge of the subject, which includes the ability to recognise patterns.
- [3] Similar comments to the previous sentence can be made about this sentence.
- [4] This sentence outlines what will occur in the following paragraphs. This creates the pleasing impression that the student is in control of the structure of their essay.
- [5] This topic sentence is also in the student's own words. It introduces the narrower focus of the second paragraph.

involves using a citation at the point where you use the words or ideas of others, and providing the full bibliographical details of the source in a bibliography or reference list at the end of your assignment. This book will not provide guidance on how to do this, as referencing guides are readily available. Simply find out what referencing style is preferred in your discipline and obtain the relevant guide.

It is important to cite only the sources you have read. Sometimes you will find a useful quotation; however, the author of the quotation is not the author of the text you are reading. For example, say the author of the text you are reading, Smith, quotes Wang, and you like Wang's words. When you incorporate Wang's words into your essay you would acknowledge that Wang was quoted by Smith (different referencing systems do this in different ways) and in your list of sources you would *only* include the reference for Smith's work. Often markers read essays which contain references to several prominent researchers only to find, after a bit of sleuthing, that the same group of researchers, and the same ideas, come from an unacknowledged Wikipedia page.

What if I accidentally use someone else's idea?

Students often worry that they will present an argument in an assignment that has been published elsewhere but which they themselves have not come across. While this does happen, the likelihood that this will lead to significant trouble is small; if ideas are similar but the essay is well researched and contains all the indicators of voice discussed in Chapter 2 (see the section titled 'Being independent'), then it is highly unlikely the student will encounter any trouble. The marker might suggest, for the sake of the student's education, that they read the sources whose opinions are similar to their own. At worst, the marker might ask the student to account for the similarity. When similarities are present in a lower quality essay in which it is harder for the marker to distinguish between the student's voice and others' voices, the marker may be less lenient, but the student will still have the opportunity to account for the similarities.

The quality and quantity of sources

The peer review process

While all information has its uses, not all pieces of information are equally authoritative. This point is implied in the Undergraduate Generic Marking Criteria for the Faculty of Arts and Humanities from King's College London. One criterion for achieving the highest marks is including in your work an 'extensive range' of sources of 'outstanding quality'. But what determines the authority or quality of a source? From an academic perspective, the best sources have been through a peer review process. The peer review process, also known as refereeing, refers to the scrutinisation by experts of a piece of work before it is published, typically as a journal article, book or book chapter.

For a journal article, the standard peer review process begins with an author sending an article to an editor of a journal who undertakes an initial review. If the editor is satisfied that the article meets the minimum requirements they will send it out to review. Usually two or more experts in the field will read the article and recommend whether it should be rejected or published. Even when the experts recommend that the article be published they will usually suggest changes. The editor then assesses these suggestions, decides which are appropriate and tells the author what needs to be done before the article can be published. The author makes these changes and resubmits the article, and the editor decides whether they are satisfied with the changes.

Journal and book publishers build their reputation on how rigorous their peer review process is. As you get to know your discipline you will come to know the most highly regarded journal and book publishers.

You can still use sources that have not been through a peer review process; however, it depends on what you do with them. A Tweet or comment made about a YouTube video could be excellent evidence of popular opinion; however, you would not want to treat either as authoritative. Also, using a non-peer reviewed source (for example, an economics article from a website) in an essay which includes 15 excellent peer reviewed sources can be acceptable; however, it would be less acceptable if an essay only contained the article and three other non-peer reviewed sources.

Finally, just because a piece of writing has been through a peer review process does not mean that it cannot be challenged. Always read with a critical eye.

The quantity of sources

It can be hard to know how many sources you should include in your essays. If there is a minimum requirement, you need to meet this to avoid a mark penalty. Yet an essay which is required to include four sources and which only includes four sources can seem rather uninspired. Even including five or six sources communicates to the marker that you have made an effort to exceed the requirements, especially when the additional sources are of good quality and from beyond the course materials. On this last point, the Faculty of Law at the University of Auckland states that the highest marks are awarded to work produced by students who have undertaken 'extensive reading beyond that which is required'. Remember that it is difficult to demonstrate understanding of your subject if your reading about the subject is limited.

The mechanics of integrating sources

This section will first discuss the three ways you can incorporate others' work into your assignments: quoting, paraphrasing and summarising. After this it will introduce reporting verbs and phrases, tools that will help you differentiate between your and others' words and ideas.

Quoting, paraphrasing and summarising

Quoting

A quotation occurs when you use the exact words of someone else. The following are some points about the mechanics of integrating quotations.

- A quotation should appear between quotation marks. There is no agreement about whether you should use single or double quotations marks. The UK tends to use single, the USA double and some countries such as Australia use both.
- There is no agreement about whether a quotation should be preceded by a comma, colon or no punctuation; often punctuation is context-dependent. There is also no agreement about whether punctuation at the end of a quotation should appear inside or outside the quotation marks. Follow the convention in your discipline.
- Quotations that run over three or four lines, or 40 words, (different style guides have different recommendations) are often presented as 'block' quotations. Quotations marks are not used, the quotation is indented on the left, there is sometimes a line break before and after the quotation, and the font size is sometimes reduced by one point.
- You can modify quotations to ensure grammatical flow and to remove inessential words. Words can be inserted using square brackets – [ ] – and can be removed using ellipses (...). Some style guides suggest that the ellipsis should also appear within square brackets – [...] – to avoid any ambiguity concerning whether the ellipsis might have been part of the original text.
- Often quotations should be introduced. More on this shortly.

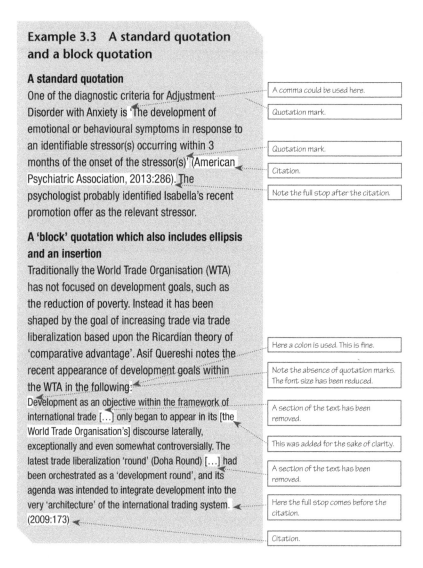

Example 3.3   A standard quotation and a block quotation

A standard quotation
One of the diagnostic criteria for Adjustment Disorder with Anxiety is 'The development of emotional or behavioural symptoms in response to an identifiable stressor(s) occurring within 3 months of the onset of the stressor(s)' (American Psychiatric Association, 2013:286). The psychologist probably identified Isabella's recent promotion offer as the relevant stressor.

A comma could be used here.

Quotation mark.

Quotation mark.

Citation.

Note the full stop after the citation.

A 'block' quotation which also includes ellipsis and an insertion
Traditionally the World Trade Organisation (WTA) has not focused on development goals, such as the reduction of poverty. Instead it has been shaped by the goal of increasing trade via trade liberalization based upon the Ricardian theory of 'comparative advantage'. Asif Quereshi notes the recent appearance of development goals within the WTA in the following:
Development as an objective within the framework of international trade [...] only began to appear in its [the World Trade Organisation's] discourse laterally, exceptionally and even somewhat controversially. The latest trade liberalization 'round' (Doha Round) [...] had been orchestrated as a 'development round', and its agenda was intended to integrate development into the very 'architecture' of the international trading system. (2009:173)

Here a colon is used. This is fine.

Note the absence of quotation marks. The font size has been reduced.

A section of the text has been removed.

This was added for the sake of clarity.

A section of the text has been removed.

Here the full stop comes before the citation.

Citation.

Example 3.3 illustrates some of the points just mentioned.

Paraphrasing

A paraphrase is produced when you present someone else's ideas in your own words. We paraphrase every day, for example, when we report what one friend said to another or what someone said on the news.
The following are some characteristics of paraphrases in an academic context.

- Quotation marks are not used, but an in-text citation is still provided.
- The length is the same as the original or shorter.
- Paraphrases are not always introduced (it is more usual to introduce quotations). However, if you regularly do not introduce your paraphrases then your voice will be diminished, especially if you use a lot of paraphrases and rarely analyse them. This was the case in Example 3.1.
- When we do not introduce a paraphrase it is referred to as 'weak author'. When we introduce a paraphrase it is referred to as 'strong author'. Example 3.4 demonstrates 'weak author' (sentence [2]) and 'strong author' (sentence [3]).

Example 3.4   An illustration of the 'strong author' and 'weak author' techniques

[1] Along with having changing definitions of what counts as friendship, older people change their expectations of the new friends they do make. [2] They expect less intimacy, shallower communication and interaction, less commitment and more casual relationships (Johnson & Troll, 1994:84). [3] Johnson and Troll also note that older people voluntarily disengage from troublesome and difficult friendships with no negative effect on their well-being (1994:80).

Students often ask how to paraphrase. However, students who are confused about paraphrasing are often not actually confused about paraphrasing itself, but are struggling to form opinions about a subject they are not familiar with. If you have read widely on a topic and have lots of interesting points to make, then putting others' ideas into your own words so they become useful for you is not particularly challenging. When you know little about a subject and have nothing to say, naturally you will feel uncomfortable as you sit there, looking up words in the thesaurus and shuffling around sentences, so that you can paraphrase your way through an essay. Importantly, what you choose to emphasise in a paraphrase (or indeed in a summary) will often depend on what you are doing with the information. This is why paraphrasing involves more than just substituting synonyms and changing the order of words. Activity 3.1, in the section 'Reporting phrases' later in the chapter, will give you an opportunity to practise paraphrasing.

Summarising

Like a paraphrase, a summary is produced when you present someone else's ideas in your own words. The following are some characteristics of summaries.

- A summary will always be shorter than the original.
- Summaries present main ideas, leaving out details and examples.
- You can summarise a paragraph, an article, a book or even a career.
- You can combine similar ideas of different authors in a single summary.
- Summaries are an excellent way to demonstrate knowledge of key aspects of another's work.
- As with paraphrasing, when summarising, quotation marks are not used but an in-text citation is required.
- It is not always possible to differentiate between summaries and paraphrases, but this does not matter. See Example 3.2 for instances of summaries.

When should I quote, paraphrase and summarise?

It can be confusing to understand when you should quote, paraphrase or summarise. This is in part because different disciplines and even teachers have their own preferences. In disciplines where word choice and phrasing are themselves frequently analysed, such as Literature, Law, History and Philosophy, quoting is more common. In disciplines where word choice and phrasing receive less attention, such as in the Sciences or Engineering, quoting is less common and sometimes even discouraged. In all disciplines paraphrasing and in particular summarising have a strong place.

Regardless of what is preferred in your discipline, quotations, paraphrases and summaries can each be used well or poorly.

- Quoting is useful when something has been said in a striking way or when you will go on to analyse word choice and phrasing.
- Paraphrasing is useful when you want to provide details of another's ideas, but you do not need to break the flow of your writing with a quotation.
- Summaries, as we have seen, are a great way to succinctly demonstrate knowledge about a subject or an aspect of it, especially because summaries can incorporate several sources. Summaries work particularly well when they appear alongside detailed analyses. The summaries demonstrate broad knowledge and the detailed analyses demonstrate detailed knowledge.

- Quotations, paraphrases and summaries are poorly used when they are too long and when there are too many of them. In both instances your voice will be diminished (see Activity 5.1 for an overly long quotation; although this is a relatively mild offender). Whether or not there are too many quotations, paraphrases or summaries is often a function of whether or not you integrate the information into your own arguments and engage with it in a thoughtful manner. Some academic work manages to convincingly incorporate many sources into relatively short paragraphs.
- Summaries can be problematic when they are borrowed from another source (such as Wikipedia) and are used to trick the marker into thinking you have read widely, when all you read was Wikipedia (see the section 'Inaccurate referencing' earlier in this chapter).

Introducing others' work: reporting verbs and phrases

Introducing others' work is useful because it allows you to differentiate between your voice and the voices of others. It can also help you to demonstrate the relationship between your ideas and others' ideas. Doing this is vital if knowledge is to be created. When introducing others' work you have many tools at your disposal. These include an abundance of reporting verbs and adverbs and a limitless number of reporting phrases you can craft which incorporate reporting verbs. Remember that a verb describes an action (Wang *argues* ...) or a state (Wang *is* happy.). An adverb modifies the verb (Wang *illogically* argues ...).

Reporting verbs

Reporting verbs indicate what others have said or done and can also indicate your attitude, or an author's attitude, to the material under consideration. These functions can help you to establish your own critical voice.

Box 3.1 provides a list of reporting verbs, categorised according to function.

Adverbs

Reporting verbs are often subtle. Occasionally you might like to add an adverb to make your attitude clear (see Box 3.2 for a list of adverbs). But be warned, adverbs should be used sparingly and only when you have good cause to do so. Consider, for example, how the tone of 'Watanabe powerfully argues that ...' is markedly different from 'Watanabe argues that ...' By using 'powerfully' you immediately position yourself as an expert, and if your analysis of Watanabe is not strong, you will end up sounding foolish.

Box 3.1   Reporting verbs

Function	Reporting verbs	Examples	Notes
Your attitude to the information is neutral	States, argues, notes, explains, points out, discusses, observes, clarifies, describes, illustrates, demonstrates, comments, mentions, presents, concludes, elaborates, believes, implies, shows, reports, adds, acknowledges, focuses on	– 'Sharma states that ...' – 'Wang elaborates on this when she explains that ...'	Much of the time you will use these 'neutral' reporting verbs.
You cautiously approve or disapprove of the information	Suggests, indicates	– 'Studies from China and the United States suggest that ...'	
Your attitude to the information is negative	Claims, asserts, assumes, believes, admits, neglects	– 'Parata claims that the integration process is far from complete; however, she neglects to ...' – 'While Fisher admits that money was wasted, she fails to...'	After indicating your negative opinion and presenting the material for consideration, it is common to use a transition signal such as 'however' to introduce your critique.
The target author's attitude to the information is positive	Urges, affirms, agrees, asserts, maintains, proves, declares, emphasises, suggests, reasons, contends, maintains, stresses, encourages	– 'Nguyen maintains that even though the evidence is inconclusive, doctors should ...'	

(Continued)

The target author's attitude to the information is negative	Doubts, disagrees, denies, challenges, concedes, questions, warns, refutes, disputes, rejects	– 'Jansen questions Trott's argument that ...'	
Something was discovered	Discovered, found, revealed	– 'The researchers found that ...'	The tense here is simple past.
These reporting verbs are informal and should only be used with caution	Says, remarks, thinks	– 'Roberts says that students are lazy.'	

Box 3.2   Some useful adverbs

Convincingly, powerfully, mistakenly, brilliantly, persuasively, ignorantly, passionately, questionably

---

Reporting phrases

Often it is not enough simply to mention an author and add a reporting verb. You might need to use additional words to ensure that the relation between your own ideas and a particular quotation, paraphrase or summary is clear. Example 3.5 contains two instances of reporting phrases in action.

Example 3.5   Reporting phrases (underlined)

1

A second function of science fiction in human development is its contribution to education. Science fiction is able to broaden the perspectives of many people. This is supported by Bainbridge's argument that 'Science fiction is a resource, offering ideas about possible courses of action and interpretations of reality' (1986, p. 156).

Analysis

Here the student combines introducing Bainbridge's argument with a link to the previous sentence.

2

According to Keynesians, as actual output begins to deviate from potential output, governments should use contractionary or expansionary monetary or fiscal policy to manage this deviation.

Analysis

'According to Keynesians' is just another way to write 'Keynesians argue that ...'

Writing and integrating paraphrases   ACTIVITY 3.1

This activity gives you an opportunity to practise writing and integrating paraphrases. Imagine you are writing a paragraph within an essay about the common errors students make when writing essays. The paragraph should warn students not to draw uncritically on their own experiences. Begin with a topic sentence that introduces the point you want to make. Then paraphrase Stott (below) and provide a negative critique of Stott's perspective. Integrate the paraphrase into your argument using a reporting verb or phrase.

Bill Stott, in his 1984 book *Write to the point and feel better about your writing*, provides the following advice:

Don't hesitate to write about what you know from personal experience. There is no stronger information. I have found many insecure writers start writing better as soon as they learn they can write about themselves without the sky falling.

Integrating figures and tables

Sometimes you will want to include graphs, charts, diagrams and tables in your essays. Box 3.3 lists the conventions you should follow.

Box 3.3   Advice for how to integrate figures and tables

- Graphs, charts and diagrams should be referred to as 'figures' and tables as 'tables'.
- Figures and tables should be numbered sequentially. Your first figure should be 'Figure 1' and your first table should be 'Table 1'.
- Figure captions are presented below the figure and table captions above the table.

(Continued)

- Your figures and tables should be given descriptive captions, that is, captions which allow the figure or table to be understood without additional explanation.
- Every figure and table included in your essay should be referred to in the text of the essay; do not leave the reader to have to work out their relevance.
- If the figure or table is drawn from another's work, reference it as you would any other source.

Conclusion

This chapter has introduced you to some of the fundamental points you need to keep in mind when engaging with others' work. It has discussed some of the ways you can avoid plagiarism, the quality of different sources and how to integrate others' work into your essays. However, knowing these basics is just the start. The real challenge is to engage thoughtfully with others' work. The following chapter will explore some of the approaches you can take and the structures you can use.

How Others' Work Can Help You Develop Your Arguments

Introduction

The previous chapter introduced you to the fundamentals of how to integrate others' work into your essays. It stressed the importance of differentiating between your voice and the voices of others and showed how you can make use of quotations, summaries and paraphrases and also reporting verbs and phrases. This chapter builds on this by explaining how others' work can help you develop your arguments. All of the approaches introduced play an important role in the process of knowledge creation. Remember that the creator of knowledge knows the ideas that already exist, understands how these ideas relate to one another and ultimately is able to evaluate and build upon these ideas. The approaches are ordered – roughly – from least to most challenging.

Eight approaches for integrating others' work into your arguments

The examples in this section draw on the five definitions of science fiction in Box 4.1. Imagine that each of the examples contributes in some way to an essay responding to the question, 'What is science fiction?'

Approach 1: Using others' work to demonstrate knowledge of a subject

Often in academic writing there is a pattern – closely related to the knowledge creation process – of first introducing others' work, then analysing it, then presenting your own point of view. This pattern can occur within a paragraph or be spread across an entire essay. Whenever you are engaged in the first part of this pattern – introducing others' work – you will be demonstrating that you have knowledge.

> **Box 4.1   Five definitions of science fiction**
>
> **Definition 1** Brian Aldiss (1973): Science fiction is the search for a definition of mankind and his status in the universe.
>
> **Definition 2** Darko Suvin (1979): Science fiction is distinguished by the narrative dominance [...] of a fictional 'novum' (novelty, innovation) validated by [...] logic. [This means that every science fiction narrative contains an innovative idea which can be explained, at least to some extent, using our current knowledge of science.]
>
> **Definition 3** David Pringle (1985): Science fiction is a form of fantastic fiction which exploits the imaginative perspectives of modern science.
>
> **Definition 4** Kim Stanley Robinson (1987): Science fiction is an historical literature ... In every sf narrative, there is an explicit or implicit fictional history that connects the period depicted to our present moment, or to some moment in our past.
>
> **Definition 5** Christopher Evans (1988): [S]cience fiction is a literature of 'what if?' What if we could travel in time? What if we were living on other planets? What if we made contact with alien races? And so on.

Example 4.1 could appear in the introduction of an essay. It begins to generate the impression that the student has knowledge by listing the authors of five relevant definitions.

Example 4.1   Demonstrating knowledge

Over the last century many definitions of science fiction have been formulated. While this essay will not be able to assess every definition, it will analyse the definitions produced by Aldiss (1973), Suvin (1979), Pringle (1985), Robinson (1987) and Evans (1988). These definitions were selected because they were written by prominent theorists, writers and editors and are indicative of the majority of definitions. Following this, a new definition will be provided which synthesises the five.

Approach 2: Using others' work to support a claim

A straightforward and commonly used way to make use of others' work is to make a claim and then support it with evidence. This evidence can include facts or the opinions of experts. You should support your claims with evidence whenever making a claim that is not common knowledge.

Example 4.2 provides a simple illustration of this approach. This and later examples could all appear somewhere in the body of an essay.

Example 4.2   Supporting a claim with evidence

Some definitions of science fiction are ambitiously brief, such as Evans' (1988) assertion that 'science fiction is a literature of "what if?"'

Approach 3: Breaking others' work into parts (the first step in analysis)

We now move to the more sophisticated approaches you can use when engaging with others' work. Typically, the first step in analysing information is breaking your information into parts. Doing this allows more precise analysis.

Example 4.3 breaks Pringle's definition into two parts. Something will be done with these parts in the following examples.

Example 4.3   Breaking information into parts

Pringle's (1985) definition of science fiction contains two related claims. First, he locates science fiction within the broader realm of 'fantastic fiction'. Second, he clarifies that the fantasy in science fiction exploits 'the perspectives of modern science'.

Approach 4: Comparing others' work

Approaches 4, 5 and 6 often occur together, but here they will be dealt with separately for the sake of clarity. As mentioned in Chapter 2, an important academic skill is identifying patterns. This can include identifying similar claims (or arguments, positions and so on) in different sources. Grouping similar claims helps you to demonstrate understanding of your subject and can also help you to support your arguments. Strong students will identify similarities which are far from obvious. If we are trying to answer the question 'What is science fiction', then identifying similarities between the above five definitions will be extremely useful.

Example 4.4 identifies two sets of similarities. The first is more obvious than the second.

Approach 5: Contrasting others' work

You can explore contrasting perspectives to demonstrate your understanding of key tensions or debates within a subject. Introducing a

Example 4.4   Identifying similarities between definitions

Similarity 1: Science fiction is a form of fantastic fiction

Looking across the five definitions we see the recurring idea that science fiction is a form of fantastic fiction. Pringle (1985) explicitly makes this point; however, it is also implied in Evans' (1988) claim that 'science fiction is a literature of "what if?"', especially because the examples he provides are fantastical. We could also categorise both Suvin's (1979) 'novum' and Robinson's (1987) 'fictional history' as 'fantastic'.

Similarity 2: Science fiction is a form of historical fiction

The definitions provided by Suvin (1979), Pringle (1985) and Aldiss (1973) can all be seen as being aspects of Robinson's (1987) claim that 'Science fiction is an historical literature'. First, any 'novum' (Suvin 1979) can be thought of as being a part of a fictional history which connects the period depicted to our present moment. This is because a novum must be able to be shown to have developed from our current scientific knowledge. A similar point could be made about Pringle's claim that science fiction 'exploits the imaginative perspectives of modern science'. Second, a useful way to understand the status of humanity in the universe (see Aldiss 1973) is to think about the trajectory of humanity. History attempts to understand this trajectory by comparing the past with the present; science fiction attempts to understand this trajectory by comparing the present with an imagined future.

contrasting perspective can also assist with making a critique.
As mentioned, a strong student will even introduce perspectives which contest their own perspective and will explain why theirs is superior.

Example 4.5 contrasts Evans' definition of science fiction with other definitions.

Example 4.5   Contrasting different definitions

From the body of the essay

Evans' (1988) claim that 'science fiction is a literature of "what if?"' implies, like many other definitions of science fiction, that science fiction is a fantastic fiction. However, unlike many other definitions (see Robinson 1987; Suvin 1979), it does not contain the idea that science fiction must in some way connect the period depicted with the present.

Approach 6: Evaluating others' work

Evaluations or critiques can be positive or negative. You can evaluate many aspects of another's work, including their reasoning, evidence, assumptions, aims, methods, conclusions, structure, expression and their own analyses. You can even evaluate the extent to which a funding source might have influenced the gathering and interpretation of data. For example, from time to time we hear that soft drink producers fund academic studies into the causes of obesity (yes, really) and the studies invariably conclude that a lack of exercise, not diet, is the problem.

Example 4.6 contains three evaluations. Note how Evaluation 1 builds on the contrasting undertaken in Example 4.5. Often, identifying a contrast is followed by an evaluation.

Example 4.6   Evaluations of others' work

Evaluation 1

Evans' (1988) claim that 'science fiction is a literature of "what if?"' implies, like many other definitions of science fiction, that science fiction is a fantastic fiction. However, unlike many other definitions (see Robinson 1987; Suvin 1979), it does not contain the idea that science fiction must in some way connect the period depicted with the present. Ultimately, Evans' definition is too broad. We can imagine works responding to questions such as, 'What if there were dragons?' or 'What if magicians really existed?' However, such works would be classified as 'fantasy' not 'science fiction'.

Evaluation 2

Robinson (1987) states that 'Science fiction is an historical literature'. While he is right that a work of science fiction must connect 'the period depicted to the present moment', as this is what distinguishes science fiction from fantasy, he should not limit science fiction to literature. The genre of science fiction should also include movies, television shows, video games and potentially other art forms.

Evaluation 3

Aldiss (1973) makes the ambitious claim that science fiction is the search for a definition of mankind and his status in the universe. While it is true that many works of science fiction are concerned with understanding the current status and, indeed, trajectory of humanity in the broadest possible terms – the movie *2001* or Lem's novel *Solaris* come to mind – others are so ludicrous (the movie *Plan 9 from Outer Space*) or so dominated by action (the movie *Mad Max: Fury Road*) that it would be hard to say they have such grand aspirations.

Approach 7: Building on others' work

Not only do stronger students compare, contrast and evaluate, they use a discussion of others' work as an opportunity to present their own ideas. By doing this, not only is the student establishing a context to which they can meaningfully contribute, they are ensuring their own ideas will be better received.

Building on others' work often follows naturally from evaluating others' work. For instance, Evaluation 2 in Example 4.6 builds on Robinson's definition by expanding the genre of science fiction to include more than just literature. And Evaluation 3 builds on Aldiss's definition by interpreting 'a definition of mankind and his status' to mean 'the current status and, indeed, trajectory of humanity'. Arguably, this alteration is more precise than the original.

Approach 8: Synthesising others' work (combining different perspectives)

To use the words of the Department of Philosophy at the University of York, Synthesis involves 'bring[ing] together material from different sources, such as different works, different authors or different parts of a course'. The outcome of this can be an improved and sometimes new perspective. Synthesising usually involves considerable analysis (breaking others' work into parts, comparing, contrasting and evaluating) and often your own original ideas will be included. Synthesis often occurs across an entire essay, that is, an essay which supports a general argument (a thesis) by analysing a range of perspectives, is engaging in synthesis.

A small thing you can do to start to bring synthesis into your work is to ensure that you use two or more different sources in at least some of your paragraphs. Essays which are dominated by paragraphs which are themselves dominated by a single source can end up being a straight regurgitation of others' ideas.

Example 4.7 synthesises the five definitions of science fiction to create a more substantial definition. It draws together much of the material from the previous examples. Some of this material is clearly present, such as the modification of Aldiss's definition that occurred in Example 4.6. Sometimes the material only informs the synthesis without being present; for example, the synthesis does not mention Evans' definition, even though the evaluation of his overly general definition inspired the decision to differentiate between fantasy and science fiction. A briefer version of this synthesis could appear towards the end of an essay as the definitive response to the question, 'What is science fiction?'

Example 4.7   A synthesis of the definitions of science fiction

[1] Science fiction is, as Pringle (1985) states, a form of fantastic fiction; [2] however, unlike some fantastic fiction, science fiction can be thought of as historical in that in every science fiction work 'there is an explicit or implicit fictional history that connects the period depicted to the present moment, or to some moment in the past' (Robinson 1987). [3] A key part of this history is the fictional 'novum' (see Suvin 1979). [4] This 'novum' (novelty, innovation) can, unlike the novelties in some fantasy works, always be explained using current scientific knowledge. [5] The 'historical' perspective of science fiction facilitates one of science fiction's frequent concerns: providing a definition of humanity, especially in relation to the universe (see Aldiss 1973). [6] By establishing a link between the present and, in most cases, a future, science fiction encourages us not only to evaluate the current status of humanity, but to reflect on humanity's trajectory.

Analysis

- Sentence [1] draws on the first part of Pringle's definition. The second part of Pringle's definition is not used because it overlaps with Suvin's definition, and Suvin's is more precise.
- Sentence [2] links Pringle's definition with Robinson's. It does this by introducing some original work inspired by the evaluation of Evans' definition in Example 4.6. The word 'literature' was left out to ensure that science fiction refers not only to books but to movies and other forms.
- Sentence [3] presents Suvin's definition as a major component of Robinson's.
- Sentence [4] paraphrases Suvin's definition and echoes the contrast between science fiction and the broader genre of fantastic fiction introduced in sentence [2].
- Sentence [5] frames Aldiss's definition in relation to Robinson.
- Sentence [6] clarifies and builds upon Aldiss's definition.

Sounds good, but I'm struggling to use all these approaches!

Naturally, it is one thing to understand these approaches and it is another thing to use them in your essays. Do not worry too much if you are not immediately able to produce complex comparisons and syntheses like those shown above. It takes time to build your skills and become familiar with your subject. And bear in mind that most student essays do not move past making claims and supporting these with evidence (Approach 2). Be satisfied if you are able to contrast two perspectives at some point in your next essay, or perhaps make one or two evaluations.

To become better at using the above approaches you need to do the same things you would do to become a better critical thinker (see the end of Chapter 2). This is because the above approaches are very much indicative of critical thinking. Once again:

- Take an interest in what you study (or study what you are interested in).
- Do (parts of) your course readings and go to class.
- Find quality sources and make good notes from them.
- Start working early.

Analysing a student paragraph

The above approaches will now be illustrated by analysing an example (4.8). The example, which is drawn from an Economics essay, combines several of these approaches. The essay question was, 'To what extent should policy be used to stabilise the economy? Discuss with examples from the UK.' This question is asking students to think about the merits of government intervention either through fiscal or monetary policy.

The paragraph is the first paragraph from the body of the essay. It is mostly concerned with demonstrating knowledge (Approach 1) rather than evaluating or making original arguments; although some evaluation (Approach 6) appears in the final sentence. More substantial evaluations and contrasting perspectives appear later in the essay. Note that the paragraph does not cite the sources of the majority of the information it presents. While this is not ideal, given that the information provided could be considered common knowledge in Economics, perhaps the approach was acceptable.

Example 4.8   A 'demonstrating knowledge' paragraph

Essay question

To what extent should policy be used to stabilise the economy? Discuss with examples from the UK.

First paragraph from the body of the essay

[1] Keynesians advocate using policy to stabilise the economy. [2] According to Keynesians, as actual output begins to deviate from potential output, governments should use contractionary or expansionary monetary or fiscal policy to manage this

deviation. [3] With respect to expansionary monetary policy, Keynesians believe that by increasing Government spending, decreasing taxes and by decreasing interest rates, recessions can be averted. [4] Consider the demand shock that occurred in 2001. [5] At this time there was a crisis in consumer confidence in the United States, a major trading partner of the United Kingdom. [6] This was due to a collapse in share valuations, a slump in the Information Communications Technology sector and the wider fall out after the events of September 2001. [7] As a result, demand for British exports fell and this had an adverse effect on aggregate demand. [8] It has been said that the effects of this depression in the US on the UK were mitigated by the decrease in interest rates in the UK from 5% in September 2001, to 4% in November 2001 and throughout 2002 [a reference to a website is provided here], thus causing output to increase. [9] This shows that stabilisation policy can be used to offset the effects of economic shocks.

Analysis

- [1] **Approach 1** The first sentence makes a general statement about Keynesian economic policy. This demonstrates broad knowledge.
- [2] **Approach 1** A summary is used to present more specific, although still quite general, knowledge.
- [3] **Approaches 3 and 1** The focus is narrowed to expansionary monetary policy. Narrowing the focus is the same as breaking into parts. Knowledge about expansionary monetary policy is demonstrated.
- [4]–[8] **Approaches 1 and 2** The student demonstrates practical knowledge by introducing an example which illustrates Keynesian theory in practice. This example is an instance of supporting a claim with evidence.
- [9] **Approach 6** The student concludes the paragraph with an evaluation; namely, that Keynesian theory can be effective. This is a good concluding sentence.

Identify the approaches used

ACTIVITY 4.1

The paragraph for this activity is drawn from the body of another Economics essay; this essay was on obesity. The essay question was, 'The rise in obesity threatens to cause a decline in age expectancy. What are the economic factors behind the rise of obesity? Is there a case for government intervention? Discuss the arguments for and against government intervention.' The paragraph is addressing the argument against government intervention. Study the paragraph and identify which of the eight approaches are used. The paragraph is more complex than the paragraph in Example 4.2.

(Continued)

Essay question

The rise in obesity threatens to cause a decline in age expectancy. What are the economic factors behind the rise of obesity? Is there a case for government intervention? Discuss the arguments for and against government intervention.

Paragraph from the body of the essay

[1] The first argument against government intervention is the frequently encountered point that this intervention will remove the consumer's right to make decisions for themselves, the idea being that this right is an indispensable component of the free-market system. [2] In an address to the Queensland obesity summit, Tony Abbott, minister for health at the time, and a proponent of the free-market system, asserted that each individual in Australia should have a sense of responsibility about the food they consume, and understand the consequences of their actions (Abbott 2006). [3] Instead of controlling the kind of food on the market, he advocated that food advertisers clearly mark on the packaging of a product the fat, sugar and sodium content in a way that is understandable, and therefore allow the public to make their own informed decisions about what they consume. [4] In contrast to Abbott's position, Gittins argues that "with such indisputable evidence that a significant proportion of people – including children – are having trouble regulating their food intake, it's simply idle to respond that they should exercise more self-control" (Gittins 2006). [5] Developing Gittins' point, it makes no sense to argue that the recent rapid rise in obesity is the result of people spontaneously ceasing to take responsibility for what they eat; this argument necessarily underpins Abbot's position. [6] Clearly structural factors are causing obesity. [7] While more substantial government interventions will be suggested below, in the least, if consumers are to make decisions for themselves, governments need to ensure that consumers have choice. [8] Such choice is currently lacking. [9] Restaurants and convenience stores, whose food is high in fat, sugar and salt (Gittins 2006), cater to those who have busy lifestyles and may often be unable to prepare their own meals at home. [10] With no choice available between unhealthy and healthy food, these people do not have the opportunity to choose their food responsibly. [11] They can only choose not to eat.

Conclusion

This brings us to the end of the two chapters about engaging with others' work. If you would like to see more complete paragraphs that illustrate different ways others' work can be used to develop an argument, Chapters 9 and 10, which deal with paragraph construction,

are worth reading. You can also study the annotated essays in
Chapter 12.

Two main points to take away from this and the previous chapter are:

- You need to integrate others' work into your essays in ways that
  preserve your own academic voice. Even if you dedicate an entire
  paragraph to introducing others' work, you still need to introduce this
  work and explain how it relates to your broader arguments.
- Use your engagement with others' work as an opportunity to
  demonstrate knowledge about and explore the complexities of your
  subject and present your own opinions.

Academic Writing Style, Grammar and Layout

Introduction

There is often debate about the extent to which writing style and grammar should matter. One argument is that so long as a person's meaning is clear, how they express themselves is not so important. While this might be true in some instances, the reality for students is that style and grammar matter very much for markers; the requirement of having good expression and grammar is present in nearly all marking criteria. Furthermore, it is rare that poor style and grammar do not inhibit clarity.

A musical analogy is useful. If your style is informal or wordy and if your writing has many grammatical errors, this is like a performer who has not practised for a performance. If your writing is incomprehensible, this is like a performer who cannot even play their instrument. Ultimately, you want your writing to have a transparent quality: the marker should grasp your meaning without even noticing they are reading. This is just like enjoying a good performance.

This chapter will identify a number of errors made by students and explain how they can be fixed. The bulk of the chapter will focus on writing style. The grammar advice will be limited to some of the most common errors. There will be a brief section at the end about how to present your essays.

Academic writing style

To understand what is special about the academic writing style we can compare it with other types of language use. A lot of the language we use every day, especially when we speak, not only conveys an obvious meaning, it indicates things like friendliness or that we belong to a certain group. Think, for example, about the additional meanings conveyed in the greetings we use: hello, good morning, hiya, g'day, hey man. We can also use language to create beauty, as occurs in poetry. However, in academic writing we try to use language which, for the most part, is stripped of these additional meanings and functions (of course, whenever you produce good academic prose you will be indicating that you are a member of a highly educated class!). There is a formal international English, albeit with some regional and contextual variations, to which we try to conform when writing in an academic context. This section will clarify the characteristics of this.

Avoid informality

In English, as in all languages, some words and phrases are considered formal and some informal. Informal language should be avoided in academic writing not only because it often performs additional functions such as indicating friendliness, but because, as is the case with slang, sometimes the meaning will not be clear to someone who is not a member of a particular group. Most of the expression problems discussed in the sections below create a sense of informality. Example 5.1 lists some informal words and phrases and their formal equivalents.

Example 5.1   Some informal words and phrases and their formal equivalents

Informal word or phrases (in italics)	Formal equivalent
The experimenters then *worked out* ...	The experimenters then determined ...
However, one key aspect of Isabella's case does not *mesh* with her psychologist's diagnosis.	However, one key aspect of Isabella's case does not support her psychologist's diagnosis.
This second argument is going to *talk* about ...	Second, this essay will consider ...
Yang is *basically saying* that ...	Yang's point is that ...
This idea *comes* from the fact that ...	This idea derives from the fact that ...
The recipients of the medication were *mixed up*.	The recipients of the medication were confused.
This fact should not be ignored *as well*.	This fact should also be considered.
One of the characteristics of a good movie is the extent to which it deals with *front-burner* issues.	One of the characteristics of a good movie is the extent to which it deals with significant issues.

Be careful when using technical terms (jargon)

Technical terms, or jargon, are words or phrases specific to an area of expertise. The meaning of these words and phrases is usually unclear to laypeople. Technical terms are useful because they allow efficient communication between experts. Examples of technical terms are 'back end' (used in computing to refer to part of an application that is not seen by the user), and 'secondary colour' (used in art to refer to colours which are created by mixing primary colours). However, technical terms can shift from being a means of making communication between experts more efficient and become a kind of formal slang, functioning to indicate membership of a prestigious group. Even worse, technical terms, when combined with wordiness, can be used to dress up weak or unremarkable arguments. That the overuse of technical terms is an enduring problem, even among academics, is implied in the 'Author Guidelines' for the academic journal *Philosophy and Literature*. There we read, '[The editors] prefer contributions free of jargon or needless technicality. Clarity is one of our ideals.' So, what should you do? In the interest of being able to communicate with as wide an audience as possible try to minimise your use of technical terms. And if you do need to use a technical term, define it.

Reflect your degree of certainty in your language

Less experienced students sometimes believe they can only make an argument if they are certain it is correct. This is not true. Often the outcome of exploring a complex problem is a statement which cautiously supports or opposes a position. The simple rule is that when your reasoning and evidence are strong, match this with language which indicates a high degree of certainty. When your reasoning and evidence are weaker, use hedging language to indicate your caution. Much of the time showing a little caution is a good idea. Hedging language includes words such as 'perhaps', 'this suggests that', 'largely', 'it is likely that', 'a little', 'generally'.

However, hedging language can also be abused. Consider the following horoscope. 'This month you may find love if you are patient.' The hedging here ensures that whatever happens the writer of the horoscope is blameless: if a person does not find love, it will be because they were not sufficiently patient; though even patience will not guarantee love. Example 5.2 demonstrates both good hedging and unhelpful hedging.

Avoid overly emotive language

Sometimes we are tempted in academic writing to express our feelings about a subject. While doing this is not forbidden, it is discouraged, unless doing so is part of the assignment (for example, a reflective essay). Remember, once again, that academic work is successful when it establishes its points using

Example 5.2   Good hedging and unhelpful hedging

1 Good hedging

Perhaps the most important role that Science Fiction can play in human development is inspiring technological advances.

Analysis

While the student's claim is plausible, many would not agree. Thus, without 'Perhaps', a reader who is knowledgeable about science fiction might be more likely to view what follows in a negative light. With 'Perhaps', the knowledgeable reader will wait to see what the student argues before making up their mind.

2 Unhelpful hedging

Stories of alien invasions seemed to dominate early science fiction movies.

Analysis

'Seemed' is a case of over-hedging. Either stories of alien invasion did or did not dominate early science fiction movies.

reasoning and evidence. Showing that you care about a subject or even that you are on the 'right' side of a debate will not gain you any marks. None of this is to say that you should not have strong feelings about what you write; rather, you should use your feelings to motivate you to track down good sources and produce compelling arguments. Example 5.3 provides an overly emotive claim and an improved version of it.

Example 5.3   Too much emotion

Emotive version

The unmitigated farce which was the Prime Minister's shabby handling of the tariff negotiations would have been laughable if the political climate had not been so serious.

Analysis

'Unmitigated farce', 'shabby' and 'laughable' all carry too much emotion.

Non-emotive version

The Prime Minister's handling of the tariff negotiations was concerning given the political climate.

Analysis

Here all of the emotive words have been replaced by 'concerning'. We now expect that further reasoning and evidence will be introduced to support the claim.

Be wary of using poetic language

Poetic or literary language creates meaning using not just the denotative or literal meanings of words, but their connotative or aesthetic qualities. Poetic language is not desirable in academic writing because it can make writing hard to follow; also, it is simply distracting. This is not to say that your writing has to be dry. A bit of creative flair can be acceptable. But your work must already be academically strong and the creative flair has to do something useful, not just seem like a poor attempt at creative flair. Too often markers encounter poorly researched and argued essays which are filled with grammatical errors and painful attempts at sounding poetic. Example 5.4 contains an instance of unsuccessful poetic language.

Example 5.4   Unsuccessful poetic language

From a student's essay
As one's art is often a reflection of oneself, the ways that extra-terrestrials have been inked onto paper and shown on the silver screen can be explored to reveal the characteristics of the creator.

Analysis
The point that a person's art reflects who they are is certainly worth exploring; however, the poetic phrases 'inked onto paper' and 'the silver screen' contribute little. Moreover, 'the silver screen' is a cliché and thus not even poetic.

To get a sense of successful poetic language in academic writing see Example 5.5. The extract comes from Hurley, Dennett and Adams Jr's book *Inside Jokes: Using Humor to Reverse-Engineer the Mind* (2011, p. 44).

Example 5.5   Successful poetic language

From an academic book
Release theories construe humor as a form of relief from excessive nervous arousal ... . Release theory [however] has lost popularity for a variety of reasons. First, in the information age, the metaphor of psychic energy, and the tensions and pressures that build up as this ghostly gasoline accumulates in the imagined plumbing and storage tanks of the mind, seems old-fashioned and naïve.

Analysis
The poetic language used here is successful in part because of its gentle mocking of the metaphors used in psychoanalysis.

Finally, some words are literary in nature and will sound annoyingly poetic regardless of how they are used, for example, 'poignant'.

Avoid clichés

A cliché is an overused expression. Clichés should be avoided for the following reasons:

- they sound informal because of their overuse, especially in speech
- their meaning can be unclear
- they make the writer seem lazy and unintelligent

Example 5.6 contains some clichés and improved versions. Technical terms can also become clichés.

Example 5.6   Clichés

Cliché (in italics)	Improved version
First and foremost, this essay will show …	Most importantly, this essay will show …
Day after day, things once thought impossible are becoming possible.	We regularly encounter things which were once thought impossible becoming possible.
The patient, Isabella, originally presented with a range of symptoms that can be *boiled down* to two core groupings …	The patient, Isabella, originally presented with a range of symptoms that can be reduced to two core groupings …
The student needs to *unpack* the term.	The student needs to explain what the term means.
These remarks are a *prime example* of …	These remarks are an excellent example of …
It is these ideas that researchers need to *bring to the party*.	It is these ideas that researchers need to include in their work.

Avoid circumlocution and tautologies (wordiness/padding and repetition)

Writing is guilty of circumlocution (or 'wordiness' or 'padding') when it uses too many words to make a point. As mentioned in Chapter 2, you should always try to say what you mean using the fewest words possible. Circumlocution can occur when a student attempts to sound 'academic' or when they add unnecessary words to reach a prescribed word count. It also arises in the normal course of drafting and should be addressed when editing. Example 5.7 contains two instances of padding and improved versions.

Example 5.7   Two instances of padding

Example of padding	Improved version
More than often the notion of X almost always means the use of Y.	Frequently X involves the use of Y.
The idea of the concept should not be understood as referring to …	The concept should not be understood as referring to …

Editing wordy prose   ACTIVITY 5.1

Read over the text below drawn from a student's essay. The essay is responding to the question 'To what extent is Science Fiction a valuable genre?' Identify redundant words and write a more efficient version. Some thoughts are provided in the Appendix.

Extract from a student's essay

[1] A second role that is played by science fiction in human development is in ideologies and education. [2] Science fiction has been able to open minds of many people around the world; telling stories about places with different rules, values and stereotypes, places where life is different, sometimes better, sometimes worse; places that make the reader think about what he or she wants in life or how to act, and ergo, help to create new ideologies. [3] This is supported by Bainbridge's argument that "Science fiction is a resource, offering ideas about possible courses of action and interpretation of reality. [4] When SF disseminates a really new idea, many people may adopt it, not because there are forced to but because they find it of value in their own life. [5] In those cases, science fiction becomes a potent cultural influence" (1986:156).

Moving to tautologies, a tautology occurs when two words mean the same thing (for example, 'ideals and values') or when the meaning of one word is implied in the meaning of another (for example, 'report back'). If you do need to clarify a point by stating it again in different words, simply flag the repetition by writing something like 'in other words' or 'that is'. Example 5.8 contains several tautologies and improved versions.

Avoid rhetorical questions

Rhetorical questions are questions whose answer is implied. They are inappropriate in academic writing because you should say what you mean, not rely on implication. Sometimes we see rhetorical questions used for dubious purposes. For example, if someone wants to be racist while

Example 5.8   Tautologies

Tautology (in italics)	Improved version
These works *share several things in common*.	These works share several characteristics.
Narrow grounds for lifting the corporate veil do exist, but judicial reaction has been seen as *inconsistent and lacks uniformity*.	Narrow grounds for lifting the corporate veil do exist, but judicial reaction has been seen as inconsistent.
This placed the *responsibility and control* over health and illness within the medical profession.	This placed the responsibility for health and illness within the medical profession.
The author writes about people who feel that their lives are *pointless and purposeless*.	The author writes about people who feel that their lives are purposeless.

retaining the possibility of denying their racism, they might ask, 'Do X really understand what it means to be Y?' (where 'X' refers to a cultural group and 'Y' to a nationality).

Be consistent with your word use

In your essays you will sometimes create your own technical terms or concepts. You will also use words that, while being non-technical, still have a precise meaning in a particular essay. It is important to stick to these words once you have introduced them. If you abandon them or start using synonyms, the reader may become confused about what exactly you are talking about. The extracts in Example 5.9 come from an essay responding

Example 5.9   Inconsistent use of terms

From the essay's introduction
This essay will argue that science fiction exploits many negative stereotypes associated with women, and because of this, it has a detrimental impact on the perception of women in society.

From later in the essay
In order to avoid being too radical, even seemingly progressive movies which depict independent women regularly include a helpless woman. Therefore, although science fiction can show autonomous women, there is always a tendency to reinforce existing archetypes.

Analysis
Straight away the marker will wonder whether the student made a mistake by writing 'archetypes' instead of 'stereotypes', or whether the student is trying to make a subtle point. The marker does not want to have to waste time and brain power pondering such things.

to the question, 'Discuss the depiction of women in science fiction.' In the course of the essay the student shifts from speaking about 'stereotypes' to speaking about 'archetypes'. This is not good.

Avoid using contractions

A contraction is a type of abbreviation where two words are shortened and combined. Contractions will not obscure your meaning; however, they sound spoken and thus informal. There is not a strong case against their use in academic writing but it is still best to avoid them. Example 5.10 includes a few common contractions to avoid.

Example 5.10   Common contractions to avoid

Do not write: It's, don't, can't, isn't, shouldn't, won't, mightn't, could've, doesn't
Write: It is, do not, cannot, is not, should not, will not, might not, could have, does not

---

Use other abbreviations, including acronyms and initialisms, appropriately

Other abbreviations you might consider using include 'etc.' (etcetera), 'i.e.' (id est) and 'e.g.' (exempli gratia). While these abbreviations are sometimes used in academic writing it is best to avoid them just to be safe. But note that nobody ever writes 'id est' or 'exempli gratia'; instead, people use 'that is' or 'for example', respectively.

An acronym or initialism is formed when the first letter or letters of two or more words are written in the place of the full words. An acronym differs from an initialism in that an acronym is pronounced as a new word whereas the initials in an initialism are articulated individually. Familiar acronyms include NATO (North Atlantic Treaty Organization) and NASA (National Aeronautics and Space Administration). Familiar initialisms include DVD (digital video disc) and CIA (Central Intelligence Agency). Some might argue that 'i.e.' is an initialism. Acronyms and initialisms are acceptable in academic writing so long as the first time they appear the full words are used, with the acronym or initialism appearing in brackets. Example 5.11 demonstrates the correct use of acronyms and initialisms.

Example 5.11   The correct use of acronyms/initialisms

First use: The North Atlantic Treaty Organization (NATO) is the dominant global military alliance.
Subsequent use: NATO was formed in 1949 with the signing of the North Atlantic Treaty.

Be wary of using 'I'

It is rare that an academic gets through a week without being asked about the use of 'I' in essays and other assignments. Unfortunately, there is no consensus about whether or not 'I' should be used. Box 5.1 contains some of the arguments against and for the use of 'I'.

Box 5.1   Arguments against and for the use of 'I'

Against	For
The reader knows you wrote the essay therefore there is no need to write 'I'.	Using 'I' is sometimes the simplest way to phrase something. It is better than referring to yourself as 'the writer' or 'the author'.
'I' should not be used because it makes your work appear subjective when it should appear objective.	Given that using 'I' only affects the appearance of your work, not the substance, it is harmless.
Avoiding the use of 'I' encourages you to be more objective.	Many successful academics use 'I' when they write, so students should not be penalised for using it.
Using 'I' is informal.	'I' is only informal when overused. Using it can make your writing more engaging.

What should you do? You should use 'I' when doing so is permitted by your discipline and marker and when it contributes to clear expression. It is also acceptable when an assignment requires a personal response, such as a reflective essay. However, 'I' can be avoided much of the time.

Example 5.12 contains an instance where the use of 'I' is unnecessary (1), where the 'I' is less problematic but nonetheless could be removed (2), and a case of a successful academic using 'I' (3).

Example 5.12   The use of 'I' in student and academic writing

1 The unnecessary use of 'I'
[1] Scholars such as Bruce Sterling take a utilitarian view of the creation of genres, which I support. [2] Sterling rightly asserts that if there is not 'a deeper social need' to create a new genre, the genre should not be created.

(Continued)

Analysis

The student makes their opinion clear in the second sentence with the adverb 'rightly', and thus the words 'which I support' are unnecessary.

2 A less problematic use of 'I'

[1] These accusations merit a thorough assessment of the current legal situation regarding lifting the corporate veil of corporate groups. [2] I will focus on this aspect of the debate in the remainder of this essay.

Analysis

The use of 'I' in sentence [2] is less problematic; although the sentence could have been phrased differently. For example, 'The remainder of this essay will focus on this aspect of the debate.'

3 An academic (Susan Moller Okin [1977, p. 345]) using 'I'

[1] While I cannot here discuss all the relevant dialogues, the following paper attempts, through analysis of Plato's arguments about private property and the family in relation to the polis, to explain why he appears so inconsistent about the nature and the proper role of women. [2] I contend that when one compares the arguments and proposals of the Republic with those of the Laws, it becomes clear that the absence or presence of the private family determines whether Plato advocates putting into practice his increasingly radical beliefs about the potential of women.

Analysis

In sentence [1] Okin could have written, 'While this paper cannot discuss' rather than, 'While I cannot here discuss'; however, perhaps she considered such wording to be less engaging. Similarly, sentence [2] could have begun with, 'This article contends that', but this wording changes little.

Grammar

As mentioned, if your grammar is very poor then your meaning will not be understood and you will likely fail your essays. Once your grammar reaches a level where your meaning is reasonably clear, grammatical errors will create a bad impression. Penalties vary depending on the marks allocated to expression and grammar and the mood of the marker. Making grammatical errors, particularly common ones that are easily avoided, are often interpreted by the marker as a sign that you do not care about your essay. Having thought this, they will view everything you write in a negative light. Remember that having a marker who feels generous when appraising your essay is an asset. As this is not a book about grammar, only a few common errors will be mentioned.

Possessive apostrophes

In English we usually form plurals by adding an 's'. Yet we can also indicate possession – that someone or something possesses something – by adding an 's'. To remove the confusion that this could cause we use possessive apostrophes. The rule is that the possessive apostrophe comes after the end of the noun, as it would be written if possession was not being indicated. Thus, if we are talking about a dog who owns a ball, we write 'the dog's ball' (there is one dog, so the apostrophe comes after the 'g'). If we are talking about two dogs who share a ball, we write, 'the dogs' ball' (there are two dogs, so the apostrophe comes after the 's').

Box 5.2 covers the main ways the possessive apostrophe should be used and when it should be avoided. The rules are straightforward except in the case of proper nouns which end in 's' (for example, Yeats, Socrates, Jones). There is no consensus about what should be done in such cases.

Box 5.2   Correct use of the possessive apostrophe

Case	Rule	Example
Singular noun which does not end in an 's'	+ apostrophe + s	The dog has a ball = The dog's ball
Singular noun which ends in an 's'	+ apostrophe + s	The bus has a wheel = The bus's wheel
Plural noun which does not end in an 's'	+ apostrophe + s	The children have a ball = The children's ball
Plural noun which ends in an 's'	+ apostrophe	Two dogs have a ball = The dogs' ball Two cities host an event = The cities' event
A singular proper noun which ends in an 's'	*either* + apostrophe *or* + apostrophe + s	Jones has a car = Jones' car *or* Jones's car Flanders has a car = Flanders' car (*not* Flanders's) (Homer Simpson always struggles with this one)
Possessive pronouns (its, his, her) do not take an apostrophe		A boy has a ball = His ball A thing has a ball = Its ball Note: It's ball = It is ball
Dates do not take an apostrophe unless ownership is implied		Correct = The 1970s were a turbulent decade for oil Correct = 2014's best movie was *Birdman*

Semicolons and colons

The battle for the correct use of semicolons and colons is being lost. Increasingly we see semicolons used where there should be a colon or comma, and the gentle art of colon use is fading.

Box 5.3 provides advice about what you ought to do.

Box 5.3   Correct semicolon and colon use

Correct use	Example
Semicolons can be used to separate two sentences which are closely related in meaning. In other words, you could also use a full stop.	The negotiations failed; it seemed there would be no end to the conflict.
Semicolons can be used before a conjunctive adverb (a transition signal). These words include 'however', 'therefore' and 'moreover', but not the coordinating conjunctions, for, and, nor, but, or, yet, so ('FANBOYS').	Modi suggested that the policy had been too harsh; however, the consensus was that the policy had been too lenient.
Semicolons should be used in a list which contains items which have internal punctuation.	The police examined the man's house; the location where he was last seen, which was also where his wallet was found; and the garage where he worked.
Use a colon, not a semicolon, to indicate that what will follow expands or clarifies what has just been written.	Trang had one desire: to come top of the class.
Similarly, use a colon to introduce a list.	Trang enjoyed the following foods: truffles, capers, olives and artichokes.

Parallelism

In academic writing sometimes we produce sentences which contain complex lists. A 'complex list' is a list whose items are not single words but phrases. The rule is that each list item (each branch of the sentence) must fit grammatically and sensically with the part of the sentence that introduces the list (the trunk of the sentence). Example 5.13 contains two cases of incorrect parallelism.

Example 5.13   Incorrect parallelism (problematic parts in italics)

1 Incorrect
The candidate's goals included winning the election, creating a national health program and *the education system*.

Correct
The candidate's goals included winning the election, creating a national health program and improving the education system.

Analysis
The 'trunk' of the sentence is, 'The candidate's goals included ...' Clearly it makes no sense to say, 'The candidate's goals included the education system.' A word like 'improving' is needed.

2 Incorrect
Over the last three decades the US has shown leadership on key issues such as the breakup of the former Yugoslavia, the war on terrorism, *its important role in the UN, World Bank and IMF, and providing financial support for developing nations*.

Correct
Over the last three decades, the US has shown leadership on key issues such as the breakup of the former Yugoslavia and the war on terrorism. It has also played an important role in the UN, World Bank and IMF, and has provided financial support for developing nations.

Analysis
The 'trunk' of the sentence is, 'Over the last three decades the US has shown leadership on key issues such as'. It makes no sense to say, 'the US has shown leadership on key issues such as its important role in the UN'.

Unclear pronoun referent

Students sometimes start sentences with pronouns such as 'it', 'they' and 'this'; however, it is not always clear what these pronouns refer to. In standard use, if we start a sentence with a pronoun we are referring to the subject of the previous sentence. Confusion can arise when we use a pronoun to refer to the object of the previous sentence or a subject from a couple of sentences earlier. If there is a possibility of confusion just restate the noun or rephrase what you are saying. See Example 5.14.

Example 5.14   Unclear pronoun referent

Unclear The car crashed into the building. It broke apart.
Clear but clumsy The car crashed into the building. The building broke apart.
Clear with improved phrasing The car crashed into the building causing the building to break apart.
Clear with improved phrasing The car crashed into the building, which broke apart.

Tense

While there are many tenses in English, there are four you will commonly use in your essays: present simple, past simple, present perfect and future simple. Box 5.4 explains and illustrates these tenses.

Box 5.4   Common tenses in academic writing

Tense and description	How the tense is formed	Example
Use *present simple* when you refer to things that have been written by others, even if they were written long ago.	Use the present tense form of the verb.	Plato *argues* that only once philosophers become rulers will states function as they should.
Use *past simple* when you refer to something that actually happened. This could be an outcome of a study or an event.	Use the past tense form of the verb.	The researchers *found* that ... In an address to the Queensland obesity summit, Tony Abbott *asserted* that ...
Use *present perfect* when speaking about recent research. This tense implies people have done things in the past and these things continue up to the present. You can also use present perfect in your conclusions.	Use has/have + the past participle form of the verb.	More recently, research *has focused* on ... This essay *has argued* that ...
Use *future simple* when you are outlining what you will go on to discuss.	Use will + the present tense form of the verb.	This essay *will argue* that ...

Other common grammatical errors and misused words

Box 5.5 lists some more common errors that markers find especially annoying.

Box 5.5   More common errors

Common error type	Advice	Example
Subject/verb agreement	In complex sentences it can be difficult to identify the subject and ensure that the verb agrees with it. In the example the verb must agree with 'The number', *not* 'The number of isolated words'.	Incorrect: The number of isolated words that a child is able to use *increase* rapidly up to the age of two years. Correct: The number of isolated words that a child is able to use *increases* rapidly up to the age of two years.
Affect/effect	Affect is usually used as a verb. Effect is usually used as a noun.	Correct: The drug affected him. Correct: The effect was large.
Their/there/they're	'Their' is a possessive pronoun. 'There' is often used to refer to a place. 'They're' = they are.	Incorrect: There research was strong. Incorrect: Their are three concerns.
Your/you're	'Your' is a possessive pronoun. You're = you are	Incorrect: Your welcome.
Who/whom	Use 'who' for the subject (when talking about he, she, they). Use 'whom' for the object (when talking about him, her, them).	Correct: Who are the people with whom we need to speak? (Ask yourself, '*Who* are the people?' The answer, '*They* are the people'. Ask yourself, 'To *whom* do we need to speak?' The answer, 'We need to speak to *them*'.)
Disinterested/Uninterested	Disinterested means unbiased. Uninterested means not interested	Incorrect: The students were disinterested in what was being taught. Correct: The students were uninterested in what was being taught.
Literally	'Literally' is overused (it has become a cliché) and regularly misused. You can write without using it.	Incorrect: Europe was literally bursting from the influx of people.

Spot the errors in expression and grammar and write an improved version   ACTIVITY 5.2

See how many errors in expression and grammar you can find in the following paragraph (yes, it is silly). Write an improved version.

Dubious paragraph
File sharing is a thing when your given access to digital movies, songs and TV shows and when you give access to you're movies, music and TV show's, and when both of you can copy the files onto their own PC or stick. Files are got on sites that let users connect with each other so that the files can be downloaded in the blink of an eye. You can go onto a site and search and look for what you want, like TV show's and movies and download them to your PC. File sharing is illegal as it goes against copyright; and those doing it are acting illegally. Do they really understand that its being illegal and evil and that it negatively effects producers? I think they need support.

Layout

Having a poor layout has a similar effect on a marker as making common grammatical errors: the marker will likely view your entire essay in a negative light. Given that there is variability in layout preferences, you should always check your university's requirements before submitting work. Box 5.6 introduces a number of aspects of layout you should keep in mind.

Box 5.6   Guidelines for presenting your essay

Layout aspect	Elaboration
Title page	Sometimes a title page is required which includes the student's name/number, the essay question, information about the course and so on. Sometimes it is enough if the essay question is included at the top of the first page and the student's details are included in the essay's header or footer.
Line spacing	Use 1.5 or double spacing. Single-spaced assignments are harder to read and write comments on.
Font	Times New Roman is often preferred. Avoid obscure fonts.
Font size	11 or 12 point is preferred.

Page numbers	Include page numbers in the essay's header or footer.
Margins	One-inch (2.5 cm) margins on the left and right of the text are usually the minimum requirement. Narrow margins make it hard to write comments when marking by hand.
Borders	Do not put borders or other decorations around your essay.
Indenting	The first line of each paragraph should be indented (press 'Tab' once).
Headings	Essays usually do not include section headings. However, they can be helpful. In the absence of headings, topic sentences perform the structural work of headings.
Reference list/ Bibliography	Present your reference list or bibliography on a new page at the end of your essay.
Print on one side only	If a hard copy is required, double siding is not preferred.
Staples	If a hard copy is required, a single staple in the top left-hand corner is preferred. Do not make your essay into a 'book' by stapling it all down one side. This is particularly annoying.

Conclusion

With expression, and especially with grammar, there is always more to say. However, this chapter has covered much of what you need to know to express yourself formerly and clearly. As a final piece of advice, even though there are not always a lot of marks to be gained in an essay for expression, grammar and layout, once you move beyond essay writing and have to write things such as thesis proposals, articles and grant or job applications, sometimes everything hinges on your expression, grammar and presentation. Clear, grammatically correct, well-presented prose creates an excellent impression, whereas even one misused possessive apostrophe can sink the ship (I have heard employers say this very thing). Therefore, use your university essays to practise getting these details right.

Chapter

6

The Essay Question

Introduction

Even though many essay questions are short, given they are the seed from which your essays grow they deserve considerable attention. Too often students hastily select a question then get on with writing their essays without thinking about what exactly the question is asking or indeed whether the question lends itself to scoring a high mark. This chapter will provide eight pieces of advice that will guide you when you are selecting and responding to essay questions. The most substantial piece of advice is presented first: 'Answer the question, the whole question and nothing but the question.' The discussion of this will include guidance about how to analyse essay questions. After this, the advice is more or less presented chronologically from the point of view of the researching and writing process.

Answer the question, the whole question and nothing but the question

Answer the whole question

A question sometimes contains two or more components and all of these must be addressed. A straightforward example of a 'piecemeal question' is the following question from a course on perception in the discipline of Psychology. 'Are there any tetrachromats? Why would we expect them to be women? How would their vision be different to trichromats?' All three sub-questions must be answered. An example of a less straightforward piecemeal question is, 'With particular reference to Iraq during the 21st century, how have parties to armed conflicts related to cultural property, particularly to World Heritage Sites, and has this been appropriate given the international laws? In your answer consider laws protecting cultural property and how they have been enforced.' The challenge with this question is not just answering all aspects of it, but finding a structure that will allow you to do this in a logical fashion (see Example 7.3 for further analysis of this question).

Answer nothing but the question

You should never include material that does not help you to answer the question. The temptation to break this rule is powerful for both weak and strong students! Often it is not until we begin to edit our work that we even notice that some of what we have written is off topic. Furthermore, relevance is not always a black and white issue; frequently students include material which is potentially relevant, but the relevance is not obvious. In these cases the marker might write, 'This is an interesting point, but you need to do more to make it obvious how it helps you to answer the question.'

Example 6.1 illustrates the problem of not answering the question. It comes from the introduction of a political philosophy essay responding to the question, 'To what extent is the quality of a society affected by the quality of its leader(s)?' Included is the essay's third point, as presented in the essay's outline. Although this third point is related to the question, it does not really help to answer the question.

Example 6.1   Not answering the question

Essay question
To what extent is the quality of a society affected by the quality of its leader(s)?

The essay's third main point
It is not only leaders but the people within a society who have a responsibility for determining the quality of their society.

Analysis
This point makes a common mistake. The question is asking about what *is* the case. The student is talking about what *ought to be* the case. A marker might write that it is one thing to say that the people have a responsibility, it is another thing to determine whether the people actually affect the quality of their society.

Question types and task words

Students can be overwhelmed by the seemingly wide variety of question types they encounter. They can be asked to 'describe', 'discuss', 'critically assess', 'evaluate', 'explain', 'examine' and so on. Fortunately, despite the apparent diversity, there is a high likelihood you will be expected to engage with the subject matter of the question in one of three familiar ways (you might like to look back at the start of Chapter 1). The three standard question types are outlined in Box 6.1.

Box 6.1   The three standard question types

Question type 1: Demonstrating knowledge

The simplest questions, which are not all that common, will only require you to demonstrate knowledge of your subject. In other words, you will need to reproduce what others have already established. An example of such a question is, 'With reference to the chapter by Paul Christopher, what principles determine just conduct in war, according to Grotius?'

Question type 2: Exploring complexity

Some questions, in addition to requiring you to demonstrate knowledge, will require you to explore the complexities of your subject. You will usually do this by comparing and contrasting different perspectives. An example of such a question is, 'Compare the methods, theories and contributions of any two psychologists.'

Question type 3: Making evaluations/presenting your own original perspectives

In addition to requiring you to demonstrate knowledge and explore the complexities of your subject, most questions will require you to make evaluations and present your own original perspectives. Remember, this is ultimately what a creator of knowledge does. An example of such a question is, 'Is social capital an analytically useful concept in relation to development?'

Be aware that sometimes a question may seem to be a Type 1 question; however, the creator of the question may nonetheless expect you to respond as if it were a Type 2 or Type 3 question. Similarly, a question which seems to be Type 2 can require a Type 3 response. See the remarks about 'Explain' in Box 6.2.

In the following tables (Boxes 6.2, 6.3 and 6.4) some of the most common task words are grouped according to question type. There are other task words, but they occur less frequently, and you should be able to deal with them based on the advice given in this section.

There is more advice about analysing essay questions in the discussion of theses in Chapter 8. There I explore the extent to which different questions lend themselves to producing theses (general arguments).

Questions without task words

Many questions do not have task words. However, you will be able to easily locate the vast majority of these questions within the above three question

Box 6.2   Question type 1: Demonstrating knowledge

Describe, outline	If you are asked to describe or outline something you are being asked to demonstrate your knowledge of facts. These facts can include specific events or relations of cause and effect. Higher-level tasks such as comparing and contrasting and evaluating might not be required. Some questions first ask you to describe or outline and then analyse, evaluate or discuss. **E.g.** Describe the diversity of the earliest members of the genus Homo. **E.g.** Describe the different models of 'birth' presented in Greek myth. Why were there so many alternatives? **E.g.** Outline Jackson's 'knowledge argument' and evaluate one argument with which a physicalist might respond.
Explain	When you are asked to 'explain' you will usually need to provide a detailed definition of a concept or a detailed account of a theory, process or why something exists or occurred. However, it is possible that in your research you will encounter conflicting perspectives, and thus your explanation may also involve comparing, contrasting and evaluating. Some questions first ask you to explain and then analyse, evaluate or discuss. **E.g.** Explain why Calvinism was the most successful brand of Protestantism in later sixteenth-century Europe. **E.g.** Explain and evaluate Foucault's views on Victorian sexual repression. **E.g.** Globally women continue to shoulder the major burden of domestic and care work in the household. How can this phenomenon be explained? **E.g.** The role of social housing in many modern welfare states is contracting and changing. Explain and analyse the changes referred to here.

types. If you like, you can even rewrite the questions using the above task words (do this in your head – do not actually rewrite them!). Take, for example, the question, 'Did the Enlightenment necessarily imply revolution?' This can be rewritten as, 'Critically assess the extent to which the Enlightenment implied revolution', or 'The Enlightenment implied revolution. Discuss.' To answer this question you would need to show knowledge of what the Enlightenment was. Some of the perspectives will

Box 6.3   Question type 2: Exploring complexity

Analyse	Analysis involves breaking information into parts and then doing something with these parts, for example comparing, contrasting, categorising and perhaps also evaluating. **E.g.** Analyse ONE or TWO plays studied this term showing how and why they can be considered examples of Naturalism or Expressionism.
Compare	Strictly speaking, comparing involves pointing out similarities; however, much of the time you should probably also point out differences, that is, 'compare and contrast'. **E.g.** Compare the 'functionalisms' of Malinowski and Radcliffe-Brown. **E.g.** Compare the impact of neo-liberal development policies in two countries from different regions (i.e. Africa, Asia, Caribbean, Latin America).
Compare and contrast	See the previous point. Note that when differences are identified between perspectives, you may also be expected to evaluate which perspective is superior, even though 'evaluation' is not implied by 'contrast'. Some questions will clearly request evaluation. **E.g.** Compare and contrast the various systems of local government revenue collection and determine which one (if any) best protects local democracy.
Show, demonstrate, account, prove	Sometimes a question will introduce an established relation between two things, concepts, theories and so on, and it will be your task to demonstrate how/why this relation exists. **E.g.** Write an essay using the ethnography, 'Traveller Gypsies', to show how ideas about dirt and cleanliness, pollution and/or taboo may be related to systems of classification. **E.g.** Account for the rise of Stalin in the 1920s.

be conflicting and in dealing with these conflicts you will be exploring complexity and will also probably need to make evaluations. You would then consider the arguments for why the Enlightenment did imply revolution and the arguments for why it did not. In doing this you would once again be exploring complexity, making evaluations and hopefully presenting your own original perspectives.

Box 6.4   Question type 3: Making evaluations/presenting your own original perspectives

Evaluate, assess, critique	These three words are closely related. All are asking you to make a judgement. A judgement can be positive or negative. All judgements should make use of reasoning and evidence.
	E.g. Evaluate the contributions made by discourse analysis and verbal report data in psychology.
	E.g. Analyse and assess the relationship between revolution and democracy in the works and deeds of Karl Marx/Friedrich Engels, Vladimir I. Lenin and Joseph Stalin.
Discuss, explore, examine	'Discuss' is a common, although somewhat vague, task word. When you are asked to discuss a subject, usually you will be expected to introduce and analyse a range of perspectives and ultimately present your own point of view. Often the task words 'explore' and 'examine' are asking you to do similar things.
	E.g. Discuss what computers cannot do.
	E.g. Explore Shakespeare's handling of the conventions of tragedy in *Othello*, and the tragedy of Desdemona.
	E.g. Examine Alfonsina Storni's treatment of gender.
Critically discuss, critically assess, critically evaluate, critically compare	Often 'critically' does not add much. Its function is simply to emphasise that you should not just describe others' work but also make evaluations. It is more useful in the case of 'critically compare'.
	E.g. Critically evaluate the evidence that different stages of sleep aid different types of learning.
	E.g. Produce a portfolio of media texts around a given topic, theme or genre. Write a semiotic commentary which analyses and critically compares your portfolio of texts.

Sometimes there is not a straightforward question

While for many essay tasks you will be asked to respond to a brief question, occasionally you will only be given a subject and it will be your job to work out which aspect of the subject you want to address and to develop your own question. When devising your question, keep in mind all the advice in this chapter.

Select/devise a question that will allow you to demonstrate knowledge and understanding of your subject

As discussed, if, in your essays, you want to generate the impression that you are a creator of knowledge, the first thing you need to do is demonstrate that you have knowledge (this is because without existing knowledge, you will have nothing to build on). This point is made by the University of Liverpool when it states that the best assignments demonstrate a command of the literature that is either broad or detailed. With this in mind, select (or devise) a question which will allow you to demonstrate your existing broad or detailed knowledge and understanding, or which relates to a subject about which you are keen to learn a lot more.

Also, most questions are written to encourage students to think about important problems and debates; usually these are introduced in the course itself. If you fail to engage with these, it is likely your mark will suffer. Thus, when selecting a question, you should ask yourself, why has this question been written? If you are unable to identify an interesting problem or debate that you can engage with, perhaps consider a different question, or speak with whoever created the question to find out what they had in mind.

Example 6.2 is concerned with how you could demonstrate knowledge and understanding in relation to specific questions. Both questions come from an undergraduate course on science fiction. Question 1 encourages the demonstration of broad knowledge about science fiction, whereas Question 2 encourages the demonstration of detailed knowledge about an aspect of science fiction and also some specific works.

Example 6.2   How to demonstrate knowledge/understanding in relation to specific questions

Question 1
What is science fiction? Discuss in relation to at least two creative works.

Analysis
The student would demonstrate broad knowledge by analysing the seminal definition(s) of science fiction and several others. Similar perspectives should be noted, as should conflicting perspectives, especially those which are indicative of enduring debates. As the question also suggests, there should be some testing of these definitions against specific works. The question asks for at least two creative

(Continued)

works to be discussed. A good student would further demonstrate broad knowledge by referring to at least five or six works. Showing detailed knowledge of particular works is not necessary. A weak response would only include one or two definitions, would not engage with seminal definitions, would not identify similar or conflicting perspectives, and would only refer to two creative works. This question probably ought to be attempted by a student who has had a long-standing interest in science fiction or who is willing to put in some work.

Question 2
Select a science fiction theme or trope (for example, aliens, time travel, dystopia). Compare two or more creative works and evaluate which provides the most convincing treatment of this theme or trope.

Analysis
For this question, the student needs to select a theme or trope about which they feel able to demonstrate reasonably detailed knowledge. This will involve having an understanding of some of the key issues and debates in relation to the theme or trope. Furthermore, the student will need to select works which lend themselves to detailed analysis of the theme or trope, and hence demonstrating detailed knowledge. Given the question's focus on detailed knowledge, the student need only discuss two creative works to do well.

Select/devise a question that will allow you to demonstrate critical thinking

As mentioned many times, one of the main things you need to demonstrate in your essays is the ability to think critically. On this point you would be wise to remember that all questions are not created equal. Sometimes your teachers will produce a range of questions with different degrees of difficulty (not always intentionally). Some questions will be easy to answer because they only require you to reproduce what others have written (they are 'demonstrating knowledge' questions), but it will be hard to score highly on them because they do not lend themselves to exploring the complexities of a subject. Questions which encourage you to explore complexities are harder to answer, but higher marks are possible.

The two questions in Example 6.3 were from an undergraduate course on international relations; they were part of a list of ten or so questions that students could respond to in their essays. One of the questions lends itself to demonstrating critical thinking, one does not.

Example 6.3   Which question lends itself to critical thinking?

Question 1
With reference to the chapter by Paul Christopher, what principles determine just conduct in war, according to Grotius?

Question 2
Why is republican government essential in order to achieve perpetual peace? Do you think it is a guarantee of perpetual peace? Discuss with reference to Kant.

Analysis
The first question only invites a descriptive response: the student is simply being asked to summarise Grotius' principles about what determines just conduct in war, based on the Christopher reading. There is no obvious room in the question for the student to explore complexity, let alone make evaluations or present their own original perspectives. The second question is a typical university essay question. First, it is asking the student to demonstrate knowledge of a particular subject: Kant's ideas about how peace can be achieved, and also his conception of 'republican government'. Second, it is asking the student to demonstrate their critical thinking skills by evaluating Kant's arguments and providing their own perspective. When presented with these two questions, undergraduate students will flock to the first question. Many will do a decent job, but even the better answers will only receive moderate marks.

Teachers sometimes inadvertently produce ambiguous questions

A point not often acknowledged in advice given to students is that sometimes students' difficulties with a question are a consequence of the question itself being poor. Remember that nothing happens to a teacher who writes a poor question, yet a student who writes a poor essay in response to a poor question gets a poor mark. A poor question can be one that, as we have just seen, does not lend itself to exploring the complexities of a subject. However, questions can also be poor because they are ambiguous. When faced with an ambiguous question, you should talk to whoever wrote the question and ask them to clarify what they meant by the question. Also, use your introduction to clarify your understanding of the question.

Be prepared to challenge the question

Some essay questions are seemingly naïve. Perhaps they make dubious generalisations. This is often done intentionally, with the hope that you will challenge the question. But sometimes the creator of the question has

Why are these questions ambiguous?   ACTIVITY 6.1

The following ambiguous questions come from courses about childhood, Australian identity and comedy respectively. Why do you think the questions are ambiguous? How might confused students have responded to these questions? How might these responses have differed from what the marker was expecting? You do not need specialist knowledge to answer these questions; the ambiguities arise from the wording of the questions.

1
How have ideas about childhood changed over the centuries?

2
The bush myth and multiculturalism have provided two highly influential ways of thinking about Australian national identity. However, these powerful concepts have also hindered our understanding of the complexity of Australian society. To what extent do you agree with this statement?

3
Drawing on theories of humour/comedy, explain why a particular funny thing is funny.

missed something. In either case, you should not be afraid to challenge the question itself. The Faculty of Medieval and Modern Languages at the University of Cambridge supports this, stating that a high-quality essay 'challenges or overturns naïve aspects of the question'. The point is that the strongest students demonstrate a high level of independence, and thus critical thinking, by challenging the very frameworks of their assignments.

Example 6.4 contains two questions which are seemingly naïve or contain naïve elements. The first, which is obviously naïve, is from a Sociology course about the way society deals with crime and punishment. The second, which comes from a course on the novel *Alice's Adventures in Wonderland*, is less obviously naïve.

Copy the question correctly

Students sometimes incorrectly copy the question when they write it on either a title page or at the top of the first page of an essay. While this error is not common, it happens enough to warrant a mention in this book! It is difficult for a marker to know what to do when a question is copied

Example 6.4   Seemingly naïve questions

Question 1

'Problems of inequality do not affect the criminal justice system in the contemporary democratic order. In law, everyone is treated equally and has equal access to justice.' Discuss.

Analysis

There would be very few people who do not think that there are problems of inequality in the criminal justice system in contemporary democracies. Thus, the function of the ostensible naïvety of the question is to provoke the student to think about some of these inequalities.

Question 2

Does fantasy simply help us to escape from reality, or does it have a more complex function?

Analysis

The question implies that using fantasy to escape from reality is a 'simple function', where 'simple function' in turn implies that this use of fantasy is banal and not worthy of investigation. A sharp student would identify and overturn this implication. They would argue that using fantasy to 'escape from reality' is actually a complex and interesting phenomenon.

incorrectly, especially when the error leads to key areas of research being neglected, or an overly simplistic or even incoherent essay being produced. Penalties will range from mild to severe.

Use the language of the question in your response

Even if you are sticking closely to the question in an essay, this will not always be obvious to your marker. To make it obvious you should use key words from the question at various points throughout your essay. Box 6.5 indicates the places in your essay where you can use key words from the question. Chapters 7–11 on essay structure will clarify many of these points.

Related to what was said in Chapter 5 about the importance of being consistent with your word use, sometimes students substitute synonyms, or even just vaguely related words, for key words in the question. They also add unnecessary words. Doing this makes their arguments harder to follow

---

Box 6.5   The places in your essay where you can use key words from the question

Introduction	• when you introduce the subject of the essay and/or the question/problem you will address • when you present your general argument (thesis) – if you have one • when you outline your main points
Body	• when you introduce what a particular paragraph will discuss • when you undertake any kind of analysis • when, at the end of a paragraph, you clarify how the content of the paragraph helps you to answer the question
Conclusion	• when you remind your reader of the question/problem addressed in the essay • when you summarise what you have argued • when you sate or restate your general response to the question

---

and ultimately makes it unclear if the question is being answered. This process of substitution and addition sometimes continues throughout an essay and by the end a student will have used several related words. If you do need to clarify or modify a key word in the question, do it explicitly. This can take the form of a definition, which, if it is brief, can be located in your introduction or in a footnote, or, if it is lengthy, can be included somewhere in the body. It can also be done in more subtle ways (see Activity 6.2 below).

Example 6.5 provides two instances, from separate essays, of students substituting synonyms for key words in a question and adding unnecessary words. The essays come from a course about childhood.

Example 6.5   Substituting and adding unnecessary words

Essay question
To what extent have people's conceptions of childhood changed over the centuries?

1 (From the introduction)
People's conceptions and beliefs about childhood are culturally determined.

(Continued)

2 (From the introduction)
This essay will argue that the perceptions about the value of childhood have radically changed through the centuries.

Analysis
In '1', not only are 'conceptions' and 'beliefs' tautological (thus 'beliefs' adds very little), 'beliefs' does not appear in the question, so there is no need to include it. In '2', the student has substituted 'perceptions' for 'conceptions' and added the word 'value'. While the question is still being addressed, the response is imprecise. The student has also substituted 'over' for 'through'. While this is a trivial change, it contributes to the impression of imprecision.

Good and bad modifications to the language of the question   ACTIVITY 6.2

The following abridged introduction is drawn from a student's essay from a course about comedy. On a few occasions the student modifies the language of the question. What do you think about these modifications? When are they successful and when are they less so? Suggest improvement. Some thoughts are provided in the Appendix.

Essay Question
Can comedy change the world?

Introduction
[1] Throughout history, philosophers and others have examined the many facets of comedy. [2] A common question which arises is, can comedy can change the world? [3] This essay argues that comedy in itself cannot cause world-wide change; [4] however, it will demonstrate that comedy may contribute to world-wide change and may also lead to change within the individual. [5] First, this essay will explore comedy's contribution to change through political satire. [6] We will see that comedy is most effective when it is a part of a broader political movement. [7] Second, and in contrast, it will discuss how comedy in fact can hinder social progression by giving people an outlet for their political frustrations. [8] Within this discussion it shall be demonstrated that comedy is part of a 'non-serious' world, and within this world progress and change is not produced[...]

Conclusion

Once again, the question is the seed from which your essays grow, and because of this, you need to take considerable care when selecting and responding to any question.

- Think about what, broadly speaking, any given question is asking you to do: is it a 'demonstrate knowledge' question, or is a more nuanced engagement with a subject being sought?
- If you do have a range of questions to choose from, choose one which lends itself to writing an essay in which you can generate the impression that you are a creator of knowledge, that is, that you have knowledge and understanding and can think critically.
- Finally, not only must you stick to the question, you must make it obvious that you are doing so.

Structure and Signposting

Introduction

Structure has already been mentioned several times in this book. We have seen, for example, that having a good structure is one of the characteristics of critical thinking. However, structure is also very much a criterion unto itself. For example, in the 'Undergraduate Generic Marking Criteria' developed by King's College London there are three main criteria: Understanding, Depth of Knowledge and Structure.

Looking in more detail at the 'Structure' criterion, we read that the best assignments are 'Excellently structured, focused and well written' and that 'Compelling arguments are made'. From this we see that structure is not just about clear organisation, but about the quality of your arguments. Building on this philosophy, in this and the following chapters, structure is rarely considered in isolation; rather, I discuss structure in relation to answering the essay question.

I break structure into two parts: 'macro' and 'micro'. Under 'macro' structure I include the generic introduction/body/conclusion structure of essays and the arrangement of points within an essay – what I refer to as the essay's 'skeleton'. Under 'micro' structure I include the structures of introductions, body paragraphs and conclusions. The first part of this chapter will focus on macro structure. It will explain why structure matters before providing some advice about how you can organise your essays' skeletons. The second part of the chapter will discuss signposting, a frequently overlooked writing tool which crosses both macro and micro structure.

Why does structure matter?

We structure information differently depending on the purpose of the information. In other words, certain structures make certain information more accessible. Think about when you go to a restaurant. Obviously, the people who run the restaurant want you to know what they serve and the price of each dish. This is done by using a menu. Usually a menu is broken into different sections which correspond with the different stages and components of a meal, for example entrees, mains, desserts, side dishes and drinks. Sometimes there are subsections within these sections which indicate the general nature of a dish, for example fish, noodles, vegetarian and gluten-free. Within these sections and subsections dishes are named and prices are given. Whereas the menu structure is useful for presenting information about meals, the essay structure is useful for exploring complex problems. And, just like a menu, some aspects of an essay's structure should always be present, while other aspects are optional.

It is also useful to compare essays with novels. This is because the comparison helps to illuminate the way essays are structured, and also because most of us learned to read by reading novels and this can cause inexperienced essay writers to produce essays that are too novelistic. Novels tell entertaining stories. Essays, once again, explore complex problems. The usual structuring logic of a novel is a sequential revelation of events: something happens, time moves on and then something else happens. The usual structuring logic of an essay is a branching argument: a general argument or thesis is supported by a number of points. It is challenging to structure an essay because, given the abstract nature of arguments, you cannot fall back on narrating events. The skeletons introduced in the sections that follow will give you a good sense of what branching arguments look like.

Generic macro structure: introduction, body and conclusion

Essays the world over are expected to follow the introduction–body–conclusion format. Because these components will be explored in detail in the following chapters, it is enough at the moment to say that the introduction introduces the reader to the question (or problem) being addressed and provides an overview of how the essay will respond to this question. The body makes detailed arguments in response to the question. The conclusion summarises what has been achieved in the body with an emphasis on how the elements within the body work together to answer the question.

The skeleton of your essay

From the moment you start to consider an essay question you should be thinking about essay skeletons. In a standard essay with a thesis (a general response to the question), there should be a clear relationship between the question, the thesis and each of the main points covered in the essay.

The thesis will often be articulated in the introduction, and each of the main points will be introduced in the topic sentences of each of your paragraphs. In shorter essays you will cover one main point per paragraph. In longer essays you might cover one main point per section, and each section will contain several paragraphs.

Examples of essay skeletons

Three essay skeletons will now be examined. The skeletons are drawn from good-quality student essays. Each skeleton includes the essay question, the thesis or general argument (if the essay has one) and the points made in the body of the essay.

Essay skeleton 1

The first skeleton (Example 7.1) is straightforward. It is drawn from an undergraduate Engineering essay responding to the question, 'What makes a professional engineer?' The essay introduces four potential characteristics of a professional engineer and explores the extent to which each is indicative of a professional engineer. The student states their overall response to the question in the conclusion, which is that a professional engineer is a combination of the four discussed points. The essay is successful not only because of its clear structure, but because it includes many thoughtful arguments in a limited space (the essay is only 700 words long).

Example 7.1   A simple essay skeleton

Essay question
What makes a professional engineer?

- **Point 1** A professional engineer has a BEng or MEng from an accredited university.
- **Point 2** A professional engineer is someone who performs work commonly recognised as 'what engineers do'.
- **Point 3** A professional engineer is a Chartered Engineer.
- **Point 4** A professional engineer is a practising engineer who acts in a morally responsible manner.
- **Conclusion** A professional engineer is a combination of the above four characteristics.

Essay skeleton 2

The second skeleton (Example 7.2) is more complex in that it makes use of sections. It comes from a Food Sciences essay responding to the question, 'Genetically modified food – are consumer concerns justified?' The essay's thesis is that a number of consumer concerns are justified, and these must be addressed; however, these concerns must be balanced against the benefits brought by genetically modified food.

Example 7.2   A moderately complex skeleton

Essay question
Genetically modified food – are consumer concerns justified?

Thesis
Consumer concerns about genetically modified food are justified, and these must be addressed; however, these concerns must be balanced against the benefits brought by genetically modified food.

Section 1
- **Point 1** The genetic modification of food is defined and described. This occurs across two paragraphs.

Section 2
- **Introduction** The three main objections to genetically modified food (GMF) are introduced: environmental risks, health risks and economic concerns.
- **Point 1** Three potential environmental hazards associated with GMF are considered: inadvertent gene transfer to other flora, reduced effectiveness of pesticides following insect adaptation to modified crops and reduced biodiversity.
- **Point 2** Three potential health risks associated with GMF are considered: an increase in allergies, unexpected long-term effects on health and inadvertent transfer of antibiotic resistance to bacteria.
- **Point 3** Two economic concerns are considered: the cost of marketing GMF and the high cost of genetically modified seeds because of the exclusive ownership of patents.

Section 3
- **Introduction** It is stated that GMF is beneficial because it can help ensure adequate food supply. Four ways adequate food supply can be achieved are introduced: enabling plants to become hardier, improving plant resistance to pests, improving storage time and enhancing plant production of vitamins.
- **Point 1** Two types of hardiness are considered: resistance to cold and drought.
- **Point 2** The main benefit of improving plant resistance to pests is considered: less pesticide can be used.
- **Point 3** The benefit of improved storage time is considered.
- **Point 4** The benefit of alleviating malnutrition through causing certain crops to produce additional vitamins is considered.

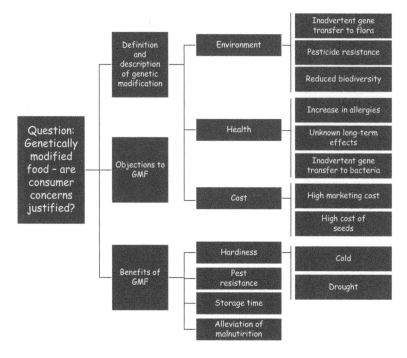

Figure 7.1 **Essay skeleton 2**

Hopefully you have noted that this skeleton makes an excellent tree diagram. The body has three main branches, with two of these branches containing further branches (see Figure 7.1).

Essay skeleton 3

Both of the previous two skeletons followed logically from straightforward questions, and it would be hard to think of better ways of structuring either essay. However, let us now consider a much more challenging question: 'With particular reference to Iraq during the 21st century, how have parties to armed conflicts related to cultural property, particularly to World Heritage Sites, and has this been appropriate given the international laws? In your answer consider laws protecting cultural property and how they have been enforced.' Following the question, an additional 13 subtopics were mentioned that students were encouraged, but not required, to engage with. Two of these were, 'The economic aspects surrounding the exploitation of cultural property' and 'International and domestic law applicable to the heritage'.

After reading the question a few times, perhaps you get the sense that a general to specific approach would be useful, and that it might make sense to begin with the end of the question and end with the beginning of the question. Specifically, the essay could begin with a more general discussion of cultural property; this discussion could engage with several of the additional 13 subtopics. Following this, the essay could consider how parties to a range of armed conflicts have related to cultural property, particularly World Heritage Sites. Finally, the focus could turn to Iraq. This was the approach taken by a high-scoring essay. The skeleton appears in Example 7.3. Note that a thesis/general argument is not included in the skeleton because the piecemeal nature of the question does not lend itself to articulating a unifying argument.

Example 7.3   A more complex skeleton

Essay question

With particular reference to Iraq during the 21st century, how have parties to armed conflicts related to cultural property, particularly World Heritage Sites, and has this been appropriate given the international laws? In your answer consider laws protecting cultural property and how they have been enforced.

Section 1 The concept of cultural property and related topics

- **Point 1** Cultural property is defined.
- **Point 2** The benefits of protecting cultural property are explained.
- **Point 3** How cultural property is protected by law is clarified.
- **Point 4** Who has the responsibility for protecting cultural property is explored.
- **Point 5** The challenges faced by parties to armed conflicts in identifying World Heritage Sites are discussed.

Section 2 Cultural property damage in recent conflicts and the responses to this damage.

- **Point 1** The conflict in the former Yugoslavia in the 1990s.
- **Point 2** The terrorist attacks in Mali in 2013.
- **Point 3** The conflict in Syria from 2012.

Section 3 Cultural property damage in Iraq in the 21st century and the responses to this damage.

- **Point 1** The damage caused and permitted by the US-led coalition is discussed.
- **Point 2** The damage caused by Islamic State of Iraq and Syria is discussed.

Developing skeletons   ACTIVITY 7.1

Come up with a skeleton in response to one of the following questions. The questions
are derived from the statements in Activity 2.1; you can draw on your responses there
for this activity. First, work out all of the points you think are worth discussing or
arguments you think need to be made. Next, work out the most logical way to
organise these. Finally, come up with a general response to the question which
encompasses all of your points.

Questions

- Is the internet good?
- Is the world becoming a better place?
- Has gender equality been achieved?

Challenges when developing an essay's skeleton

When developing an essay's skeleton you need to negotiate four challenges.

(1) Points are abstract and thus structuring them can be challenging

As mentioned, points are abstract, meaning they exist out of time. You will
thus need to come up with a structuring logic and be able to explain, at
least to yourself, why you have chosen it. This can be relatively easy when
the structure is given to you in the question, such as with the question,
'What is humanitarian intervention? Should humanitarian interventions
occur?' However, sometimes you might need to do quite a lot of reading
and planning before you work out the ideal structure. Sometimes you can
draw on standard structures. Some of these include:

- moving from the general to the specific
- making strong arguments followed by weak arguments
- making arguments in favour of something then arguments against
  something
- presenting information then critiquing information

(2) The hierarchy of your points needs to be appropriate

You need to work out whether particular points you want to make are
thesis-level points (your general response to a question), main points (you
might have three or four of these in an essay) or subpoints (you might
have two or three of these in a section or paragraph). Sometimes when
you are planning an essay you will think that a point you want to make is
very important, only to discover, upon writing, that it is minor.

(3) There should be minimal overlap between your points

It can be hard to avoid repetition because points frequently overlap. If this overlap cannot be avoided, use appropriate signposting to flag the overlap. For example, 'Building on the previous point ...'

(4) Where relevant, you should maintain structural parallelism

Imagine you are analysing two different techniques for solving a problem. When discussing the first technique you begin by describing the technique, then you say what is good about it, then what is bad about it and suggest what changes should be made if any. You should follow the same structure when discussing the second techniques.

Signposting

The idea behind signposting is that if you want your writing to be easy to follow, not only do you need to arrange your ideas logically, you need to indicate this logic to your reader. Or, as an ex-student of mine recently tweeted, *make points, relate points.*

Signposting has already been mentioned in the discussion of how you can keep your voice strong (see p. 17). There is a close link between the two topics because when you take care to lead your reader through your arguments you are making yourself clearly present. Reporting verbs and phrases are also signposting (see Chapter 3). This section will briefly outline all the forms signposting can take. Most of the points will be taken up again in the following chapters.

A small caveat: signposting can be overdone. Signposting should be used to make your arguments easier to follow, it should not be used indiscriminately. It is usual to include a lot of signposting – especially transition signals (joining words) – when drafting and to remove some of these in the editing process.

Introductions, including topic sentences

Introductions point towards what you are going to argue in your essay or a part of it. The importance of introductory signposts is indicated in the 'General Guidelines' from the School of Philosophy, Psychology and Language Sciences at the University of Edinburgh. Under 'Structure' we read, 'Does each part of the essay/exam have a clearly indicated purpose?'

In longer essays you should not only have an introduction at the start of your essay (see Chapter 8), you should include brief introductions at the start of each section. Section introductions can often take the following form: 'Having explored X, we now need to consider Y for reason Z. This shall be done by focusing on A, B and C.'

Topic sentences are introductions for individual paragraphs. It is rare that they are not used. Topic sentences introduce the point (subject or argument) to be covered in the paragraph and can also provide a link with what has just been said (see p. 108).

Conclusions, including concluding sentences

Conclusions point back to what has been achieved in your essay. Their focus should be on summarising what was argued and how this contributes to answering the question (see Chapter 11).

Sometimes it can be good to finish a paragraph with a concluding sentence which clarifies what has been achieved in the paragraph as well as the paragraph's relevance to the broader argument being made and/or the question (see p. 112).

Transition signals

Transition signals are the joining words which indicate the relation between the parts of a sentence, two sentences or two larger blocks of writing. They can be a single word ('however' or 'furthermore'), a phrase ('in more detail') or even a sentence ('Having considered X, we now need to consider the broader issue, Y'.) (see p. 110).

Reporting verbs and phrases

When you introduce someone else's work you are signposting that your voice is about to stop and someone else's voice is about to start. When introducing someone else's work you can also clarify the relation between this work and your own (see Chapter 3).

General linking

The final type of signposting is general linking. General linking occurs whenever you link a discussion in one part of your essay with a discussion elsewhere (for example, 'Earlier we saw that ...', 'Related to the previous point ...'). It is usually a way of managing overlap between points. If you do not flag this overlap the marker may find the overlap uncomfortable. By drawing attention to the overlap, not only is the overlap usually forgiven (markers are aware that overlap is often unavoidable), you will be awarded marks for self-awareness and having a clear structure.

Conclusion

A key point to take away from this chapter is that structure is one of the main challenges of essay writing. If, when you are writing your essay, you find yourself stumbling from one paragraph to the next, not knowing where you are going, then it is likely you have started writing too soon and have not given enough thought to how your points will be organised. Even a bad plan is better than no plan at all. This is because a bad plan can be modified. As mentioned, as you become a more experienced writer, when you first read a question, not only should the complexities of the subject fill your mind, you should begin to think about possible skeletons. The other point to take away is that good signposting complements good structure. You might see the structure of your work in your head, but if your reader cannot see it then the benefits of having a good structure will be lost.

Essay Introductions

Introduction

Introductions provide the reader with an overview of what will occur in the body of the essay. To explain why they exist, it is again worth comparing essays with novels. Novels are written to entertain, and one of the main ways they do this is by creating mysteries. Essays are not written to entertain, but to demonstrate knowledge, explore complex problems and, at higher levels, create knowledge. Given this, it makes sense to avoid mystery and provide an overview of the essay at the outset. Or, in the parlance of our times, to start an essay with the 'spoiler'.

However, there is no such thing as a 'right' introduction. Students and academics in different disciplines achieve success using different structures, and different questions sometimes require different approaches. This chapter will provide advice about how to construct a *comprehensive* introduction, but because the information will be presented in a modular fashion, you will be able to adapt the advice to suit your needs.

Broadly speaking, an introduction should respond to three questions: '*What* question or problem is being addressed, *why* is it significant and *how* will the essay respond?' The key functions of a comprehensive introduction follow from these. A comprehensive introduction will:

- introduce the subject being addressed and provide some contextualising information
- indicate why the subject is significant
- introduce the specific question or problem being addressed within the subject
- indicate why the question or problem is significant
- present a general response to the question or problem (this is the essay's 'thesis' or 'main argument')
- outline how the essay will be structured

A well-written introduction conveys to the marker that you understand the task you have been set and that you have thought carefully about your subject and arguments. It is also a useful resource when reading your essay: the marker can always return to it to be reminded about what you are trying to achieve and how the components of your essay fit together. So, begin well and the marker will look favourably on all that follows. Begin badly and your essay may never redeem itself!

The orientation

Common orientation elements: subject, question/problem, significance

Use the beginning of your introduction, which will be referred to as the 'orientation', to introduce the subject of your essay and then the question or problem you will address. Remember that a question and a problem are the same thing, only the phrasing is different. By moving from making general remarks about a subject to introducing the question/problem, you are 'funnelling' your reader into your essay. To mix metaphors, this helps the reader know where to 'file' the specific information in the essay.

When I say 'introduce the subject', I do not mean you should write, 'This essay will focus on X' (though doing this would not be disastrous – at least it is to the point). Rather, you should present some contextualising facts, key tensions and so on. As you will see from the examples in this chapter, this can be done in many ways. When introducing the subject and the question/problem, you should indicate why both are significant. This can be done subtly (again, see the examples). Remember, any reader will want to know not just *what* you are writing about, but *why* you are writing about it. By including this information you will be demonstrating understanding of your subject.

Example 8.1 is a good orientation. It is drawn from an essay in the discipline of Health. The essay was responding to the question, 'How can Sociology and Psychology help health and social care professionals to understand the experience of health or the effects of illness/disability/service delivery on the individual?' The essay was 3000 words; thus the orientation is longer than would be expected for a 1500- or 2000-word essay.

Optional extras: scope and definitions

Scope

At the end of your orientation, or perhaps later in the introduction (see Example 8.2), you might like to include some remarks about your essay's scope. The scope of an essay refers to what is included and what is left out. Sometimes questions are intentionally broad to encourage you to focus on an aspect of a subject that interests you, or to test if you are able to identify key issues. When faced with a broad question, you could write something

Example 8.1   A good orientation

Essay question

How can Sociology and Psychology help health and social care professionals to understand the experience of health or the effects of illness/disability/service delivery on the individual?

Orientation

[1] When modern medicine was established in the nineteenth century it was based upon the premise that illness was caused by diseases attacking the body. [2] Health was believed to be the absence of disease. [3] Health care was therefore based almost entirely upon the conceptualisation of health as a biological state of being. [4] Society as a whole and the individual's psychology were believed to have little or no influence over health, illness or disability. [5] This placed the responsibility and control over health and illness within the medical profession. [6] This view of health has since been described as the medical model. [7] In the twentieth century sociologists and psychologists began to challenge the medical model of health. [8] They suggested that health is influenced by society and individual psychology as well as biology. [9] Sociology and psychology explained not only the effects of society and the individual on health but through scientific studies developed theories which explained the experience of health and the effects of illness, disability and service delivery on the individual.

Analysis

The orientation locates the essay question within the broader history of modern medicine. The orientation also gives us a good sense of the tension between the 'medical model' of health and more contemporary models which take account not just of biological, but sociological and psychological, factors (see sentence [4]). By drawing attention to this tension the writer is indicating the significance of the question; namely that sociological and psychological perspectives about health and illness can be valuable tools for health and social care professionals. Note that the history elegantly culminates with a statement that is closely related to the question (sentence [9]). We now expect the introduction to introduce the specifics that will be covered in the essay. Altogether this orientation provides a strong illustration of 'funnelling'.

like, 'While this essay could discuss W, X, Y and Z, it will focus on Z, as in recent years this topic has garnered much controversy.' By mentioning W, X, Y and Z you are *flagging* that you are aware of the range of topics that could be covered; this demonstrates that you have broad knowledge of your subject. By narrowing the scope you are ensuring that the content of your essay is manageable. By justifying your decision you are demonstrating self-awareness and thus critical thinking. All too often markers are presented with essays that either try to cover too much or that focus on one or two specific points for no obvious reason.

The following instance of scope narrowing (Example 8.2) is drawn from the introduction to a Sociology essay concerned with how societies deal with crime and punishment. The essay question, which we saw in Chapter 6, was, '"Problems of inequality do not affect the criminal justice system in the contemporary democratic order. In law, everyone is treated equally and has equal access to justice." Discuss.' As many topics could be discussed, it makes sense that a shorter essay (in this case 1500 words) would need to narrow its scope. The example includes the student's thesis (general argument) and the scope narrowing which follows.

Example 8.2   A good narrowing of scope

Essay question

'Problems of inequality do not affect the criminal justice system in the contemporary democratic order. In law, everyone is treated equally and has equal access to justice.' Discuss.

Thesis and scope (the orientation is omitted)

[1] In contemporary society, inequality in the law does exist; which is to say, not everyone is treated equally, nor does everyone have equal access to justice. [2] This inequality is manifested in many ways across democracies. [3] For instance, we see it when some use their wealth and understanding of the legal system to avoid or delay justice. [4] We also see it in a range of situations amongst the disadvantaged and marginalised within a society. [5] Given the limited space, this essay will focus on the latter, in particular the inequalities experienced within Australia by migrants, specifically those from non-English speaking backgrounds, and Indigenous people.

Analysis

- [1] The student provides a succinct general response to the question.
- [2] The scope narrowing begins with a general statement which demonstrates that the student has thought broadly about the question.
- [3]–[4] The general statement is substantiated with two examples.
- [5] The scope is narrowed to an aspect of the second example. Interestingly, in this introduction this narrowing of the scope also functioned as an outline (the introduction finished at the end of sentence [5]).

Definitions

Sometimes introductions can contain definitions. A definition is useful when it clarifies the meaning of an uncontentious technical term in a concise manner and when doing so, in turn, helps to clarify the problem being addressed by the essay. We see this in Example 8.3. This example contains the first part of an orientation from an Economics essay. In the example there are three definitions of uncontested technical terms: one in the text itself and two in footnotes.

Example 8.3   An orientation with well-integrated definitions

Essay question

To what extent should policy be used to stabilise the economy? Discuss with examples from the UK.

Orientation

[1] Stabilisation policy is 'short term intervention by the Government, either to counter balance some trend in an economic variable or to speed up (slow down) its natural time path' (Shone 1984:182). [2] It is used because economic variables such as output and unemployment in the short term deviate from their long-term potential and natural rates respectively, creating a so-called business cycle. [3] The source of these deviations and the way Governments respond to them leaves a lot to argue about ...

Analysis

'Stabilisation policy' is defined in sentence [1], and 'potential rates' and 'natural rates' are defined in footnotes (these are not included here). These definitions help to clarify the problem being addressed by the essay, that is, it is important to establish what stabilisation policy is and explain why it exists before considering the extent to which it should be used. Sentence [3] is funnelling the reader towards the question and indicating that the student is aware of the complexities within the subject.

Definitions can also help to establish an essay's scope. For the question, 'To what extent is the quality of a society affected by the quality of its leader(s)?' it would be useful to clarify what you understand to be meant by 'leader(s)'. 'Leaders' could be limited to political leaders, or could include corporate and cultural leaders, or even leaders within the household. Such a scope-establishing definition would be generated by the student themselves: it need not come from a dictionary or some other source.

Definitions can be unhelpful when a term is defined that does not need to be defined because reasonable people (the readers of your essays) already know its meaning. A definition can be particularly damaging when the essay itself can be thought of as a 'definition' essay. In such an essay, at least part of the essay task will request that the essay discusses the meaning of a term. For example, 'What is meant by ergonomics and why is it central to good modern design?' or 'To what extent has the conception of childhood changed over the centuries?' Brief definitions of 'ergonomics' or 'childhood' in the respective introductions would likely be oversimplifications and as such may well conflict with later discussions. Finally, when defining terms, be wary of dictionary definitions. Dictionary definitions sometimes do not deal with the complexities of a term. Draw your definitions from academic sources.

Things to avoid when writing orientations

Orientations are weak when:

- they are only tangentially related to the question
- they are overly general and banal
- they get caught up in lengthy arguments or analyses

The weak orientation in Example 8.4 is drawn from an essay written for a course on the novel, *Alice's Adventures in Wonderland*. The essay question, 'To what extent is Alice a role model for young women?' encourages students to think about the complexities of Alice's character; these complexities are worth exploring, as arguably they have contributed to the book's enduring popularity. After the weak orientation an improved version is included.

Example 8.4   A weak orientation

Question
To what extent is Alice a role model for young women?

Orientation
[1] *Alice's Adventures in Wonderland*, published by Lewis Carroll in 1865, is a story about a little girl who falls down a rabbit hole and enters a fantasy world. [2] Once in this world she meets many unusual characters and has many adventures. [3] In 1951 the animation *Alice in Wonderland* was released by Walt Disney production.

Analysis
Sentences [1] and [2] are overly general and banal.
Sentence [3] is irrelevant.

(Continued)

Improved version

[1] One of the most intriguing aspects of Lewis Carroll's *Alice's Adventures in Wonderland* is the character of Alice herself. [2] Alice, unlike many traditional young female characters, is confident and even at times brash. [3] While a superficial interpretation of these 'strong' characteristics might lead us to conclude that Alice is indeed a role model for young women, a closer examination reveals that Alice is an ambivalent character.

Analysis

- [1] The orientation gets straight to the point, namely the intriguing nature of Alice herself. The word 'intriguing' helps to establish the significance of the subject.
- [2] This sentence elaborates on the first sentence and reinforces the idea that a study of Alice's character is significant by highlighting the fact that Alice is not a typical traditional female character.
- [3] This sentence begins to give us a sense of the complexities of the subject and provides a transition to the thesis (general argument), which, we imagine, will appear in the next sentence.

But do I really need an orientation?

Orientations in one form or another regularly appear in articles and books written by academics. This is because academics are not given a question to answer. Instead, they have to come up with their own question or problem and establish its significance. Because students are provided with the question they need to answer, they can, in theory, dispense with the orientation and begin by saying what they will argue/discuss in the essay. However, given the importance in higher-level academic work and in the professional world of identifying significant problems, you might as well practise writing orientations in your essays.

Analyse the orientation   ACTIVITY 8.1

The following orientation comes from a Corporate Law essay. The issue being addressed is the limited liability status of companies. 'Limited liability' refers to the arrangement whereby debts incurred by a company remain with the company and are not transferred to the individual shareholders of the company. Analyse the orientation. Identify the stages it moves through and explain how it engages with the question. Does it do a good job?

Essay question

In what circumstances is the judiciary prepared to relax the doctrine of the separate legal personality of a company? Is the current legal situation satisfactory from a policy point of view, particularly in the light of the group structure of many modern businesses?

Orientation to the essay

[1] The limited liability company has become the flagship of most capitalist economies since its inauguration in the nineteenth century. [2] However, business practices have changed dramatically over the past century. [3] A number of factors, such as globalization and intensified competition, have triggered the emergence of corporate groups. [4] The existence of corporate groups has arguably led to an increase in cases where the limited liability of companies has caused undue hardship for creditors. [5] The judiciary has been prepared to relax the doctrine of the separate legal personality of a company in certain circumstances and render shareholders personally liable (this relaxation is more commonly known as "lifting" or "piercing" the "corporate veil"). [6] However, the key question, which this essay will address, is whether courts have been able to satisfactorily cope with the commercial developments of the last century.

The thesis

Having introduced the subject of the essay and the question or problem to be addressed, a comprehensive introduction will next say what is going to happen in the essay. Two approaches are possible. In the first, you state, as clearly and succinctly as possible, your general answer to the question. This is the essay's 'thesis'. In the second, you do not state a thesis, but instead outline how your essay will unfold. The approach you should use will depend on the question and also what is done in your discipline.

Stating a thesis in the introduction

Many introductions state a thesis for the straightforward reason that most essay questions require a general answer. Frequently, marking criteria will indicate that a thesis should be present. For example, in the marking criteria for the Philosophy course, 'Morality & Value', at the University of Edinburgh, it is stated that in the better essays, 'A thesis/position is indicated and clearly defined.' By including a thesis in your introduction and sticking to it throughout your essay, you will be *sustaining an argument*. That this is desirable is reflected in criteria developed by the Philosophy department at the University of York. We read that one of the fundamental requirements is that essays 'Develop a sustained line of argument'. Keep an eye out for theses when you read academic articles; you will often find them in the first few paragraphs. See, for example, the introduction by Okin in the activity at the end of the chapter.

Before more is said about theses, two types of questions will be examined: questions which clearly invite a thesis (Example 8.5) and questions which possibly invite a thesis (Example 8.6). Questions which do not invite a thesis will be considered in the next section.

Example 8.5   Essay questions which clearly invite a thesis

1 An essay question from Social Psychology
Should we be worried about the effects on children of aggressive images on film and television?

2 An essay question from Politics
Is increased globalisation a good thing?

Analysis
For both questions it is obvious you should answer 'yes', 'no' or 'to some extent', 'to a small extent' and so on. Naturally, your answer will be supported by a thorough exploration of the different perspectives that exist within the respective subjects.

Example 8.6   Essay questions which possibly invite a thesis

1 An essay question from Computer Science
Discuss what computers cannot do.

Analysis
If there are a number of discrete things that computers cannot do, then at best you could state a 'list thesis'. Something like: 'This essay will demonstrate that currently computers cannot perform four classes of activities: A, B, C and D; however, with advances in technology, activities C and D could be performed in the future.' A 'list thesis' lies somewhere between a thesis and an outline, and indeed, the two could be combined. However, perhaps an enlightened student might find a way to unify all of the things computers cannot do.

2 An essay question from Business
What best describes people's willingness to work hard?

Analysis
This is a tricky one. 'Best' implies there is one reason which is superior to the others. Yet a good essay would undoubtedly consider a number of reasons, and moreover, our intuition tells us that people's willingness to work hard derives from a combination of factors. A good thesis would probably say something about this combination and perhaps would also identify the most influential factor.

Now for some more details about theses. To create a thesis you need to consider all of the specific points you would like to make (or do make – often you only work out your thesis after writing your first draft) and produce a statement that encompasses them while also answering the question. Remember to use the key words from the question in your thesis to make it obvious that you are indeed answering the question. Sometimes your thesis will be one sentence; sometimes you might need two or three sentences to ensure your thesis is faithful to the complexities of your individual points. Your outline, which will follow your thesis, can also reveal some of these complexities.

Some markers like the thesis to be signposted with words such as, 'This essay argues that'. This makes it obvious that your thesis is your thesis. Other markers believe that such signposting makes your writing seem artificial. If you have to choose, pick clarity over style.

Even though your thesis should present a general argument, this argument need not be black and white; in fact, *it probably should not be*. This is because, as discussed many times, essay questions are usually devised to encourage you to explore the complexities of a subject. So do not worry if you cannot find the 'right' answer. There probably is not one.

Example 8.7 illustrates a strong thesis. The essay question is drawn from a course in Biochemistry.

Example 8.7   A strong thesis

Essay question
Are GM crops the solution to the world's food problems?

Thesis
This essay argues that genetically modified (GM) crops are not necessarily the solution to the world's food problems. GM crops continue to help to alleviate starvation and improve health by increasing yields, reducing production costs and providing important nutrients. However, concerns remain about whether GM crops

(Continued)

will, in the long term, cause lasting damage to biodiversity or interact with the food chain in unforeseen ways. These concerns relate to the science behind GM crops, but also to how GM crops are used.

Analysis
This thesis is strong because it demonstrates an awareness of the debates within the subject and provides a clear, while nonetheless somewhat circumspect, answer to the question.

Theses are weak when:

- they are too black and white
- they do not argue anything
- they do not answer the question

The theses in Example 8.8 illustrate these weaknesses. All are responding to the following question from a course in Political Philosophy. 'To what extent is the quality of a society affected by the quality of its leader(s)?'

Example 8.8   Weak theses

Essay question
To what extent is the quality of a society affected by the quality of its leader(s)?

Thesis 1
The quality of a society is completely determined by the quality of its leader(s).

Analysis
This 'black and white' thesis is undesirable given that the question is very much encouraging a 'grey' response. The thesis gives the impression that the complexities of the subject will not be explored.

Thesis 2
This essay will discuss the extent to which the quality of a society is affected by the quality of its leader(s).

Analysis
This thesis merely reproduces the question without making an argument. This might be acceptable if the general response appears in the conclusion; however, it will not be acceptable if your marker is expecting a thesis in your introduction.

Thesis 3
In almost every society leaders are not sufficiently concerned with the welfare of the general population. Thus the world needs leaders of greater quality.

Analysis

This thesis makes a worthy argument; however, this argument does not answer the question. Specifically, while the thesis contains the assumption that leaders are able to affect the quality of their societies, it seems to be responding to the question, 'Assess the quality of contemporary and historical leaders.'

Not stating a thesis in the introduction

There are two reasons not to state a thesis in the introduction. The first, as I began to discuss in the previous section, is practical: whereas many essay questions readily lend themselves to stating a thesis, some do not. The latter include 'demonstrating knowledge' or 'piecemeal' questions. Example 8.9 contains two questions that do not lend themselves to stating a thesis.

The second reason why your essay may not contain a thesis is more philosophical. Some academics worry that encouraging students to adopt

Example 8.9   Essay questions that do not lend themselves to stating a thesis

1 An essay question from Biochemistry

By what biochemical means do athletes seek unfairly to enhance their performance? How do the authorities attempt to detect them?

Analysis

This question is inviting the student to demonstrate knowledge of the subject rather than make a general argument. A thesis would contribute very little.

2 An essay question from Developmental Psychology

A subpopulation of children with conduct problems shows temperamental differences and deficits in how they process emotion, and are described as "callous-unemotional". What are the implications for understanding the development of antisocial behaviour in children? What are the implications for diagnosis and treatment of childhood disruptive behaviour disorders?

Analysis

This question does not invite a thesis because there are three questions. The first is about understanding development, the second about diagnosis and the third about treatment. You could still give your general responses to these questions in your introduction, but these responses ought to be a part of your outline.

a position in their introductions causes them to approach their essays with closed minds. These academics are concerned that students might begin the essay writing process by coming up with a thesis and then simply finding evidence to support it, without considering whether the thesis is appropriate. For these academics, the structure of an essay should mimic the optimal intellectual journey taken by a student when writing the essay. Just as a good student will not fix their opinion until they have understood the complexities of their subject, the unifying argument of the essay should only appear after all of the salient points are introduced and dispassionately considered. The introduction for such an essay would thus contain only an orientation and an outline, and the essay's overall argument – the equivalent of a thesis – would not appear until the conclusion. I will say a few more words about this in Chapter 11 when I discuss why conclusions exist.

However, presenting a thesis in an essay's introduction need not prevent a nuanced engagement with a subject. Thinking about the research/ writing process, you should ideally start your research with a sense of what your thesis might be, but also with an open mind. As you research your subject, your thesis will develop: you might find ideas that complicate your thesis (which is good), or even challenge it, such that you need to alter it (which is also good). Your essay, then, presents two things. First, your thesis is the position you arrived at *after* carefully researching and considering your topic. Second, the body of your essay is a representation of *how you came* to your thesis: it is where you explain the ideas you found most compelling and rebut those that were interesting but which you believed to be incorrect.

As a final thought, if writers only presented their main arguments for the first time in their conclusions, readers may well begin by reading the conclusion first. This being the case, there is no reason not to include the main argument in the introduction.

Rank the theses   ACTIVITY 8.2

The following four theses were drawn from essays from a course on Australian identity. Rank the theses from worst to best. Take into account the extent to which each answers the question and prepares the way for a nuanced engagement with the subject. Some thoughts are provided in the Appendix.

Essay question
To what extent is Australian identity now based on images and ideas that relate to the beach and suburbs rather than the bush?

Thesis 1 This essay argues that the Australian identity is still based in images that relate to the bush.

Thesis 2 This essay will argue that to a considerable extent *images* of Australian identity now feature the beach and the suburbs rather than the bush. However, the *idea*, central to the bush identity, that only some Australians are 'real' Australians, continues in the two newer identities.

Thesis 3 In recent years, the media's portrayal of Australia has changed because of shifts in ideology.

Thesis 4 This essay argues that to a significant extent Australian identity is now based on images and ideas that relate to the beach and the suburbs rather than the bush. This is because the beach and the suburbs more accurately represent the diversity of contemporary Australian society and this has altered Australian identity itself.

The outline

The outline is the third main component in a comprehensive introduction. It provides an overview of the main topics you will explore and/or the individual points you will make. It should be obvious how the points in your outline help you to answer the question and support your thesis (if you have one).

As with the thesis, it is possible to use signposts to help identify the outline as an outline and to help the reader navigate the outline. You can use language such as 'First ... Second ... Third ...' or 'To begin ... Following this ... Finally ...' However, once again, some markers might not like such overt signposting and you may need to find more subtle ways of laying out your argument.

In shorter essays (around 1000 words), each point in your outline will correspond with each of the paragraphs in the body of your essay. There can even be a similarity between the wording of the points in the outline and the topic sentences of your paragraphs. For longer essays, the points in your outline will more likely correspond with sections within your essay.

See Example 8.10 for an illustration of an outline.

Final points about introductions

Length

For shorter essays (1000–2000 words), aim for you introductions to be 10 per cent of the total word count. For longer essays, your introductions should be less than 10 per cent of the total world count. To put it precisely, the length of an introduction in proportion to the total essay length should decrease as the essay becomes longer. But in any case, always try to be as economical as possible. When introductions become too long, it becomes difficult to distinguish them from the body of the essay, making them less useful.

When should the introduction be written?

Some academics advise that an introduction should be written after you have completed a good draft of your essay. Their rationale is that only once you have written the draft will you be clear about what exactly you are arguing. This is a good point; although it is nonetheless useful to *attempt* to write your introduction before you start your essay, while nonetheless being prepared to modify it throughout the writing process as your ideas develop. This preliminary introduction is your essay's skeleton (or plan), in that you are sketching the general argument you want to make and how your points will develop.

Complete introductions

It is now time to analyse a compete introduction (Example 8.10). The introduction, which is strong, comes from an essay written for the already mentioned course on *Alice's Adventures in Wonderland*. This time the question is, 'How do the Alice novels engage with nineteenth-century ideas about childhood?' The question requires the student to understand the debates about childhood in nineteenth-century England and to locate the novels within these debates.

Example 8.10   A complete introduction

Essay question
How do the Alice novels engage with nineteenth-century ideas about childhood?

Introduction
[1] During the nineteenth century, England experienced unprecedented political, religious, and philosophical debate about the roles and rights of children. [2] This was, in part, spurred by revelations of the hardships faced by children as a consequence of the industrial revolution. [3] Often at the heart of the debate was a conflict between Romantic notions of childhood innocence and Augustinian ideas of original sin (Shuttleworth 2004, p.110). [4] Lewis Carroll can be located on the Romantic side of this debate. [5] His novel, *Alice's Adventures in Wonderland*, conveys his belief that a

praiseworthy innocence is the defining feature of childhood. [6] Furthermore, Carroll utilises Alice's adventures to present the transformation from childhood to adulthood as a degenerate process. [7] First, this essay discusses some of the realities of nineteenth century English childhoods and the ideas associated with them, with a focus on the Romantic idea of childhood innocence. [8] Second, it shows how Alice's initial state of mind in *Alice's Adventures in Wonderland* reflects Carroll's belief in children's inherent innocence. [9] Third, it discusses how Alice's repeated failed attempts to remember her education are a strong critique of the non-Romantic approach to education. [10] Finally, this essay analyses Carroll's perspective that a loss of innocence is a lamentably inevitable aspect of life; [11] this will be explored by examining the development of Alice's character and some of the poems in the novel.

Analysis

- Sentences [1]–[3] orient the essay. The essay gets right to the point in sentence [1] by introducing the fact that there was debate about childhood in nineteenth-century England. By saying that this debate was unprecedented, the significance of the subject is established. Sentence [2] provides background information which builds the impression that the student has broad knowledge. Sentence [3] narrows the focus by clarifying the nature of the debate mentioned in [1].
- Sentences [4]–[6] are the essay's thesis. Carroll's general perspective is introduced followed by some elaboration. Importantly, even though the question ostensibly encourages a 'list thesis', the student has found a way to unify their response by, to use the student's words, locating Carroll on the Romantic side of the debate.
- Sentences [7]–[11] provide an outline of the essay. Throughout, the student sticks closely to the question.

Analyse the introduction

Now it is your turn to analyse an introduction. Rather than providing an introduction from a student essay, an introduction from an academic article has been selected. Okin's 'Philosopher queens and private wives: Plato on women and the family' (1977, p. 345). This introduction was selected so that you can see that even academic articles include the components introduced in this chapter. Remember that because there is no given question, academic articles must establish their own problems to solve. Some thoughts are provided in the Appendix.

(*Continued*)

Introduction

[1] Plato's ideas about women have attracted considerable attention in the last five years. [2] This is not surprising, since his proposals for the education and role of the female guardians in Book V of the *Republic* are more revolutionary than those of any other major political philosopher, not excluding John Stuart Mill. [3] However, Plato on the subject of women appears at first to present his reader with an unresolvable enigma, especially when his other dialogues are taken into account. [4] One might well ask how the same, generally consistent philosopher can assert, on the one hand, that the female sex was created from the souls of the most wicked and irrational men and can argue, on the other hand, that if young girls and boys were trained identically, their abilities as adults would be practically the same. [5] How can the claim that women are "by nature" twice as bad as men be reconciled with the radical idea that they should be included among the exalted philosophic rulers of the ideal state?

[6] While I cannot here discuss all the relevant dialogues, the following paper attempts, through analysis of Plato's arguments about private property and the family in relation to the polis, to explain why he appears so inconsistent about the nature and the proper role of women. [7] I contend that when one compares the arguments and proposals of the *Republic* with those of the *Laws*, it becomes clear that the absence or presence of the private family determines whether Plato advocates putting into practice his increasingly radical beliefs about the potential of women. [8] Only by examining the proposals of *Republic* V in the context of the overall aims and structure of the ideal society, and by doing likewise with the contrasting proposals regarding women in the Laws, will we find the differences intelligible.

Conclusion

Box 8.1 summarises what has been discussed in this chapter from the perspective of what you should include, perhaps include and not include in your introductions.

Box 8.1   Things to include, perhaps include and not include in your introductions

	Do	Optional	Do Not
Orientation	– Introduce your subject – Introduce the question (or problem) you are addressing – Mention why the subject and/ or the question is significant	– Include brief definitions of uncontested technical terms – Indicate the scope of your essay	– Be overly general or banal – Include dictionary definitions of contested terms which require considerable exploration
Thesis	– State your general answer to the question in no more than a few sentences – Be as precise and economical as possible without oversimplifying	– Use signposting language such as 'This essay argues that …' – Omit a thesis if one is not called for by the question	– Get caught up in making long, complex arguments; save these for the body
Outline	– Offer the reader a map of your essay – Ensure there is a clear link between the outline points and the question and your thesis	– Use signposting language such as 'First … Second … Third …' or 'To begin … Following this … Finally …'	– Go into too much detail; you just need to briefly indicate the structure of your essay

Rules for Writing Body Paragraphs

Introduction

In many ways we now come to the main event of this book. This is because the bulk of your essays will comprise body paragraphs (hereafter I will write 'paragraph', not 'body paragraph'). Compared with introductions, however, the structure of paragraphs is much more variable. But this is not such a bad thing, as this is where the art of essay writing really makes itself felt! This is where *you* must make decisions about how best to present the knowledge you have gained and make your arguments. Having said this, there are a number of guidelines which can help you improve your paragraphs. This chapter will discuss a number of these. The following chapter will introduce some of the many ways you can structure your paragraphs.

Ensure the content of the paragraph is relevant and useful

As has been said several times now, if what you write does not obviously help you answer the question and does not support your thesis (if you have one), then you should not be writing it. Unfortunately, it is the lot of all writers to put energy into producing text which must, in the end, be discarded.

Also, an argument may be relevant but still not particularly useful. This can be for two reasons. First, the argument may be obvious to the point of banality. For example, students who are struggling to work out what to write sometimes resort to saying things like, 'But different people have different opinions so it is difficult to say what the truth really is.' This is often correct, but saying this does not score any marks. Second, arguments are sometimes made without having a sense of proportion. Thus, while the argument might be good, the student will waste too many words on it, when they should move on to another argument. Sometimes markers receive essays which clearly answer the question, but which only provide, say, two long-winded points, and because of this the essays neglect to cover important aspects of the subject. Of course, students can also be guilty of not going into sufficient detail when making an argument.

Be mindful that your paragraphs are not too short or too long

On the internet, particularly in news articles and opinion pieces, people write using one and two sentence paragraphs. This technique works well for short pieces where the aim is to present facts, but it is not suited to essay writing which is concerned with making complex arguments. A typical essay paragraph will include a topic sentence and an elaboration upon this which can include examples, analysis and counterpoints. By grouping these elements together in a paragraph the function of each element is clearer. If each element was a separate 1–3-sentence paragraph it would be harder for the reader to follow how a particular point was being developed. Undesirable short paragraphs are called 'paragraph fragments'.

Example 9.1 contains two paragraph fragments from an essay on law and investment in Asia. The section of the essay from which the fragments were drawn was titled, 'Getting government business'. There is nothing wrong with the content, and given the close relationship between the two fragments – the first sentence reads as a topic sentence – the two could have been combined to form a single paragraph.

Example 9.1   Paragraphs fragments

Government, as well as government agencies and state-owned enterprises generate significant amounts of business for advertising firms through, for example, promotions of public health issues, marketing of government-run telecommunications companies, and advertising for state-owned airlines.

Whether advertising agencies are selected directly, through panels, or by tender, significant opportunities for corruption of public officials exist. One unnamed CEO of an international ad firm operating in Indonesia described corruption as 'endemic' in the sector and advised agencies to 'avoid government pitches' and to 'stay well clear of state-owned firms' (Mumbrella 2014). While Ad X will not exclude government as a client, it will be strict. For example, during the tender process, no gifts will be permitted.

While there is no strict upper limit for paragraph length, a paragraph should only be longer than 300 words with good reason. A typical problem for all writers occurs when they wish to make a point that contains four subpoints, where three of the subpoints are short and one is long. Ideally, you would have one paragraph, but the lengthy fourth point prevents this. It is acceptable to opt for two paragraphs so long as you signpost this decision; for example, you could label your subpoints 'first', 'second', 'third' and 'fourth'.

Have the general paragraph structure of topic sentence(s) followed by elaboration

Think of your paragraphs as being mini essays that have a one- or two-sentence introduction followed by elaboration. The topic sentence(s) will introduce the topic to be explored or the argument to be made in the paragraph. It can also provide a link with what has just been said. As discussed in Chapter 7, your topic sentences, along with the question and your thesis, should form the skeleton of your essay; thus, it is good to have some link between individual topic sentences and the question and your thesis. Also mentioned earlier, your topic sentences, especially when they introduce major points, can be similar to the points in the outline in your introduction. When a paragraph lacks a topic sentence, the reader will ask themselves, 'What is this paragraph about and how does it relate to the rest of the essay?'

The best way to get a feel for topic sentences is to see them in action. Example 9.2 includes all of the topic sentences from a short (1500-word) Sociology essay on the subject of inequality in the criminal justice system. We saw this essay question and the essay's thesis and scope in the previous chapter. An abridged thesis and scope are reproduced here.

Example 9.2   All of the topic sentences from a short essay

Essay question
'Problems of inequality do not affect the criminal justice system in the contemporary democratic order. In law, everyone is treated equally and has equal access to justice.' Discuss.

Thesis and scope
In contemporary society, inequality in the law does exist; which is to say, not everyone is treated equally, nor does everyone have equal access to justice. While this

inequality is manifested in many ways in different democracies, this essay will focus on Australia and the inequalities experienced by migrants, specifically those from non-English speaking backgrounds, and Indigenous people.

Topic sentence 1 For migrants to Australia from non-English speaking backgrounds (NESB), inequalities in the criminal justice system can stem from a number of factors. The first is unfamiliarity with policing procedures, and not knowing their rights and not being able to communicate during those procedures.

Topic sentence 2 The inequalities experienced by NESB migrants from ethnic minorities do not end at the policing level of law. Once in the criminal justice system, migrants' knowledge of the legal aid resources available to them is poor.

Topic sentence 3 Due to these difficulties, migrants are also less likely to seek legal representation as they move through the justice system.

Topic sentence 4 Language issues also contribute to Indigenous Australians experiencing inequalities in the criminal justice system. In a legal context, there are features of Aboriginal English that are particularly relevant, these being the use of silence when answering questions and also the use of 'gratuitous concurrence'. Silence is often used by speakers of Aboriginal English to think about the proposition being put forth and to become comfortable with the social situation they are in.

Topic sentence 5 As mentioned, another language barrier that leads to injustices within the criminal justice system is 'gratuitous concurrence'.

Topic sentence 6 Inequalities in the criminal justice system in relation to Australian Indigenous people are also created through differential policing in relation to Indigenous youth.

Analysis

Not only does the essay unfold logically, the topic sentences regularly include signposts which link the current paragraph with what has just been argued. Furthermore, the language of the question is regularly used to make it obvious that the question is being answered. Also, note that sometimes it takes two or three sentences to introduce the topic. For example, 'Topic sentence 4' needs three sentences to funnel the reader down to the point of the paragraph. This is because 'Topic sentence 4' also functions as a mini introduction to the second part of the essay.

A topic sentence can sometimes be omitted when a paragraph is closely related to the preceding paragraph. This can occur when a paragraph is presenting an example or a counterpoint. However, even in such instances, some kind of signposting is usually helpful, namely a transition signal such as 'for example' or 'however'. Sometimes the concluding sentence of the preceding paragraph functions as the topic sentence of the paragraph. This is demonstrated in Example 9.3, which is drawn from a Psychology essay. The essay is concerned with assessing a diagnosis. The example reproduces the last two sentences from the paragraph with the concluding sentence and the first three sentences from the following paragraph.

Example 9.3   A concluding sentence functioning as the topic sentence of the following paragraph

… Isabella does show several symptoms concordant with a diagnosis of Adjustment Disorder with Anxiety such as "marked distress that is out of proportion to the severity or intensity of [a] stressor" and "significant impairment in social, occupational, or other important areas of functioning" (American Psychiatric Association, 2013). However, one key aspect of Isabella's case does not support her psychologist's diagnosis.

One of the diagnostic criteria for Adjustment Disorder with Anxiety is "The development of emotional or behavioral symptoms in response to an identifiable stressor(s) occurring within 3 months of the onset of the stressor(s)" (American Psychiatric Association, 2013). The psychologist probably identified Isabella's recent promotion offer as the relevant stressor. However, Isabella's case points to an earlier event, during a class presentation in high school, as the beginning of her anxiety attacks…

Ensure there is a logical flow within your paragraphs and signpost this with transition signals

A considerable portion of your essay mark will be determined by how well you elaborate your arguments within your paragraphs. Elaborations need to be logical and this logic needs to be obvious to the reader. In elaborations there are a handful of typical manoeuvres, for example providing examples, reasons, introducing additional information, introducing contrasting perspectives, showing cause and effect and making evaluations. Most of these typical manoeuvres can be easily signposted with a word or phrase. These words and phrases are often referred to as 'transition signals' (we have already seen longer transition signals used to link paragraphs in Example 9.2). Without appropriate transition signals, even a logically structured paragraph can read like a collection of loosely related bullet points.

However, like most good things, transition signals can be overused. Sometimes it is obvious how a sentence elaborates on the previous one (look at the relationship between this sentence and the one before it; I did not need to write 'This is because' before 'Sometimes'). When elaborating, it can be enough to have a clear subject at the start of the sentence (or use a pronoun like 'this') which links with some aspect of the previous sentence. Box 9.1 lists some common transition signals.

Box 9.1   Common transition signals

Function	Transition signals
Indicating a sequence of events or points	To begin, then, next, following this, finally, first, second, third, the first argument, a useful starting point is, this second line of argument assumes that, one argument for X is, another argument for X is, the first thing that must be noted is
Adding information	And, in addition, moreover, further, furthermore, also, we also see that, another, consistent with the previous point, returning to the earlier argument that, as mentioned above, elaborating on the previous point, not only does X do Y it also does Z
Comparing	Similarly
Clarifying	That is, in other words, to clarify, to put this another way
Going into detail	In more detail, specifically, in particular
Providing an example	For example, for instance
Indicating a contrasting perspective	However, although, nevertheless, on the other hand, but, yet, whereas, while
Showing cause and effect or a logical relation	Because, as, then, so, thus, therefore, hence, consequently, since
Introducing a conclusion	Thus, therefore, hence, in conclusion, as can be seen, this essay has explored X
To summarise	In summary, in sum, in short, altogether
Showing a condition	If
Focusing attention on something	With respect to, with regard to, regarding, for

The paragraph in Example 9.4, which comes from a Management essay, contains a number of transition signals. The transition signals are highlighted in bold. The first sentence in the paragraph is referring to leadership styles that were discussed in the previous paragraph of the essay.

Example 9.4   A paragraph with transition signals

Essay question
Are some forms of leadership more effective than others?

A paragraph from the body of the essay
Although these leadership styles are cited as more effective, they are often subject to failure **if** used individually or in inappropriate contexts. **Thus, while** authoritative leadership is especially effective in situations where the company has lost its direction and needs a reinstating of its priorities and goals, it will not be effective where the leader's colleagues have more expertise or qualifications. Over-aggressiveness is **another** risk in using the authoritative form of leadership; it may undercut enthusiasm. Goleman (2000, p. 84) **also** notes that the affiliative style of leadership should not be used alone **as** its excess may obstruct accomplishing tasks; **specifically**, the overuse of praise may give rise to the misconception that high quality work is not required. **Furthermore**, in a complicated or difficult situation, this style of leadership may throw the group into disarray. **On the other hand**, a powerful form of leadership may be obtained by using the authoritative and affiliative leadership forms in conjunction, **so as** to provide direction while maintaining enthusiasm and encouraging flexibility (Goleman 2000, p. 85). There are **also** problems with the democratic leadership style. These arise when employees are not experienced enough to provide opinions. **Moreover**, this style of leadership can be manipulated to delay important decision making. **This** may cause the group to lose direction. **Another** significant concern is that this style is not suitable in times of emergencies, where it might be difficult to obtain majority agreement. **As for** the coaching form of leadership, this method would not work with employees who are not willing to change (Goleman 2000, pp. 85–87). **From these points we can see that** there is no simple way to speak about effective forms of leadership; effective leadership often involves combining leadership styles in a context-sensitive manner.

Include concluding sentences when appropriate

It can be a good idea to finish your paragraph by clarifying how what has been discussed helps you answer the question and/or supports your thesis. Doing this often follows naturally from analysis within the paragraph.

Though keep in mind that sometimes a concluding sentence will be overkill, meaning that your marker will think you are being repetitive or stating the obvious. Concluding sentences are less appropriate in paragraphs which present information (descriptive paragraphs), or when the topic sentence already makes it clear how the paragraph answers the question and supports the thesis. The main thing to avoid when finishing your paragraph is leaving the marker thinking, 'Yes, yes, but so what? How does this help?'

The paragraph in Example 9.4 has an effective concluding sentence. The concluding sentence does a good job of showing how the discussion in the paragraph contributes to answering the question. The paragraph in Example 10.3 in the next chapter is an example of a paragraph which does not have and does not need a concluding sentence.

Be cautious when including others' words or ideas in your topic sentences

A common way that students diminish their voice and make the structure of their essays harder to follow is by starting their paragraphs with a quotation or paraphrase, or perhaps also a summary. The 'plagiphrase' in Chapter 3 (see p. 22) is an example of this (naturally matters go from bad to worse when the whole paragraph is no more than a series of paraphrases and quotations). Beginning paragraphs with someone else's words or ideas can also encourage the bad habit of dedicating each of the paragraphs in an essay to a different researcher rather than structuring the essay around your own arguments. Such an essay effectively becomes a series of summaries. If you do include others' work in your topic sentences, make sure that you are still obviously controlling the flow of your essay.

Example 9.5 contains the first three paragraphs (only the first sentence of the third paragraph is reproduced) from the body of a Psychology essay responding to the question, 'In what sense can we speak of animals having culture?' This is an interesting question because of the common belief that human behaviour is largely the product of culture and animal behaviour largely a product of genetics. The first paragraph introduces and illustrates a basic way in which animals can be said to have culture. The second paragraph builds on the first point by identifying how the first point is deficient. The third paragraph illustrates the second point. What is noteworthy is that all three paragraphs include paraphrases or summaries in their topic sentences. The question we need to ask is, is this appropriate?

Example 9.5   Including others' work in topic sentences

Essay question

In what sense can we speak of animals having culture?

From the beginning of the body of the essay

A simple form of social interaction is when species learn via patterns of behaviour; this could be considered culture (Byrne et al, 2004). White et al (2000) presents an example of patterns of mate behaviour which are transmitted from one female quail to another. A focal female is exposed to two types of males with a test female watching. After viewing the mating the test female has to choose a mate for herself. Results showed the test female was more likely to copy the mating preferences of the focal female, suggesting that females make the same choices they have seen others make, and so show patterns of social learning behaviour. It could be said that we can speak of animals having culture at what appears to be a low level of cognitive ability.

Byrne et al (2004) stress that to define culture as a pattern is not acceptable because it does not take account of the cognitive capacity of a species, something they propose is necessary for animals to be assessed as having culture. Perhaps a definition of culture requires behaviour to be acquired such that different types of cultural traditions can exist within the same species and within the same environment (Boesch et al 1998). This could be associated with higher levels of cognitive ability because within one species different groups have developed different cultural methods to solve the same problem.

Whithen (2005) and Boesch et al (1998) noted that ant catching techniques used by Tai forest chimpanzees differ from chimpanzees that live at Gombe.

Analysis

The damage done by including others' work in the topic sentences is not serious, but improvements are nonetheless possible. On the positive side, the student's voice remains quite strong throughout:

- The relationship between the three paragraphs is clear and logical and each paragraph is itself reasonably clear and logical.
- Even though the first two topic sentences contain summaries, both topic sentences clearly engage with the question.
- The first and second paragraphs have good analysis/concluding sentences which integrate the material in the paragraph into the broader discussion.

The possible improvements are as follows.

- The second paragraph could have begun with the transition signal 'However'. Adding this would have improved the reading experience by signalling that a refutation of the previous point was about to occur.
- The third paragraph would have benefited from better linking with the end of the previous paragraph. For example, 'Whithen (2005) and Boesch et al (1998) <u>identified this phenomenon when they found that</u> ant catching techniques used by Tai forest chimpanzees differ from techniques used by chimpanzees that live at Gombe.' Note that this kind of linking takes place in the second sentence of the first paragraph.
- Given that the material in the three paragraphs follows the pattern of claim followed by illustration, paragraph three could have been combined with paragraph two.
- A more general point is that the marker might be concerned that even though there are a variety of sources in the paragraphs, the two main points both seem to come from Byrne et al.

Ensure there is only one point per paragraph

A recurring error in student essays is including more than one point per paragraph. This can occur when a paragraph falls into a narrative-like mode and one point to drifts into another. It can also occur when a student attempts to deal with too much in a paragraph. In both cases the trick is to identify the two or more main points being made and separate them. However, the 'one point per paragraph' rule is flexible. Sometimes it makes sense to include four subpoints in a paragraph, whereas sometimes it would be better to deal with each of these in a separate paragraph. Sometimes it makes sense to present both a summary and a critique in the one paragraph, whereas sometimes they should be spread across two paragraphs. Solving these problems is part of the art of essay writing.

The paragraph in Example 9.6 is drawn from the body of an essay responding to the previously seen question, 'What is humanitarian intervention? Should humanitarian interventions occur?' It is weak because it attempts to address three points rather than one. Not only is it hard to follow, the points are not sufficiently developed. A template for how the points could have been better addressed is provided after the analysis.

Example 9.6   A paragraph which suffers from including more than one point

Essay question

What is humanitarian intervention? Should humanitarian interventions occur?

A paragraph from the body of the essay

[1] Those who oppose the practice of humanitarian intervention (HI) argue that despite its professed peaceful intent humanitarian intervention involves the use of military force, and related to this, HI contravenes the international commitment to refrain from the use of force. [2] HIs end up enacting what their supporters claim they wish to prevent (Bello, 2006). [3] Specifically, HIs do not promote human rights values but instead enforce them. [4] However, HI should not be misunderstood as referring only to the use of force, as its essence lies in the idea that when interventions occur, they utilise all prevention and protection measures available, not only force. [5] People opposed to HI do not object to saving lives but rather concentrate on its illegitimacy and the debatable motives of intervening states, as interventions never occur for purely humanitarian reasons.

Analysis

- [1] Two points are introduced in the topic sentence. There should only be one point.
- [2]–[3] These sentences elaborate on the first point from the topic sentence.
- [4] A counterpoint is provided. This is good, but too brief.
- [5] The concluding sentence begins by reiterating the second point in the topic sentence (this point was not developed in the paragraph) and introducing a third point.

Template for an improved version

There are a number of objections to the practice of humanitarian intervention (HI). The first is that despite the claim that humanitarian interventions are concerned with promoting peace, they achieve this end by using force. [This point could be developed by presenting reasons and evidence to demonstrate how the use of force in HIs can undermine the pursuit of peace. Counterpoints could be presented. The paragraph could conclude by stating whether this first objection is reasonable.]

The second objection is that HIs run counter to the international commitment to refrain from the use of force. [This point could be developed by detailing the international commitment to refrain from the use of force and explaining how HIs violate this. Counterpoints could be presented. The paragraph could conclude by stating whether this second objection is reasonable.]

The third objection is that even though HIs are in principle conducted for good reasons, states only become involved with them when their own, not necessarily humanitarian, interests are served. [This point could be developed by presenting reasons for and evidence of states using HIs to pursue their own interests. This could be followed by a discussion of the mechanisms present in the international community to mitigate this. Once again, the paragraph could conclude by stating whether this third objection is reasonable.]

Avoid unnecessary repetition between and within paragraphs

Repetition takes three forms:

- Returning to a point that was addressed in an earlier paragraph. I touched on this when I spoke about 'general linking' in Chapter 7. The point made was that if repetition cannot be avoided, it should at least be flagged using language such as, 'Returning to point X ...'
- Repeating yourself either from one sentence to the next, or at different points within a paragraph. This repetition is often a result of insufficient editing. All writers repeat themselves when drafting their work; diligent writers recognise this repetition when editing and do something about it. Usually this involves deleting or combining sentences, or restructuring a paragraph. If you do wish to make the same point using different words to clarify your meaning, write 'in other words'. See Example 9.7 for an instance of repetition in an academic book.
- Repeating yourself from one word to the next. When two words mean the same thing it is referred to as a tautology. Tautologies were addressed in Chapter 5 (see p. 52). They can be easily fixed by deleting one of the two words.

Example 9.7   Repetition in an academic book

An extract from the book *Punk Sociology*
However, this chapter is not going to rehash the history of punk, this has been covered many times in the past (the key work here is the insider account offered by Jon Savage, 1991). Punk has been well documented and these histories do not need to be reiterated. There is no real point in reproducing such histories here ...

Analysis
The author makes the same point three times. Once is enough. Also, the comma after the first 'punk' should be a full stop or semicolon.

Maintain a good balance between your voice and others' voices

This point has already been covered in some detail, especially in Chapters 3 and 4. So here I will just remind you that the two main pillars of essay success are demonstrating knowledge and critical thinking and that it is hard to do one without the other. Thus, while there is no strict rule for how many sources you should include in one paragraph, it is good not to string together too many paragraphs that are dominated by others' ideas, or are heavily reliant on a single source. Nor is it good to have too many paragraphs that only contain your own ideas.

Analyse the body paragraph ACTIVITY 9.1

Analyse the following paragraph from the beginning of the body of the essay. It is responding to the question, 'Why do we like to laugh?' In you analysis, consider each of the nine points covered in this chapter. Some thoughts are provided in the Appendix.

Body paragraph

[1] The first reason we like to laugh is because of the relationship between laughter and superiority. [2] According to Aristotle and Plato, people laugh at others' misfortunes and shortcomings (cited in Bardon 2005, p. 3). [3] The reason people laugh at others' misfortunes and shortcomings is because they are not the one who suffered, and by pointing out the failures of others, they have a sense of superiority. [4] An example of this is laughing at grammatical mistakes made in formal situations. [5] People who spot the grammatical errors feel superior, or to be more specific, smarter than the parties who make the errors, and express this feeling through laughter. [6] Hobbes suggests that humour exists for letting people compare themselves with the belittled party (cited in Hurley et al 2011, p. 40). [7] An example of this is drunk people doing foolish things. [8] This example is funny because people compare themselves with the people who suffer and feel superior. [9] However, something may not be funny if the event results in serious injuries. [10] For example, it is not funny if a drunk person falls heavily onto the ground and loses consciousness. [11] And yet, if we fear that a serious injury has occurred then find that it hasn't – the drunk person gets up and is fine – we may laugh for another reason: relief. [12] This will be explored next.

Conclusion

To conclude this chapter, the aspects of paragraph writing that have been covered are arranged in a table (Box 9.2) based on the extent to which each aspect should inform or feature in your body paragraphs.

Box 9.2   The extent to which each aspect should inform or feature in your body paragraphs

Always
Ensure the content of your paragraphs is relevant and useful.
Ensure there is a logical flow within your paragraphs and signpost this, when appropriate, with transition signals.
Usually
Ensure that your paragraphs are not too short or too long.
Have the general paragraph structure of topic sentence(s) followed by elaboration.
Have one point per paragraph.
Maintain a balance between your voice and the voices of others.
Sometimes
Include concluding sentences.
Include others' work in your topic sentences, but only if doing so does not diminish your voice.
Rarely
Repeat yourself between and within your paragraphs.

Chapter 10

Different Body Paragraph Structures

Introduction

There are many ways to structure paragraphs in the body of your essay. Because of the great variety, I will not attempt to give an exhaustive account of different structures. Instead, and consistent with my approach throughout this book, I will establish some of the principles which should inform your thinking about body paragraph structures (hereafter I will write 'paragraph', not 'body paragraph'). Having done this, I will analyse a number of examples. No activities are included in this chapter because the complete essays in Chapter 12 will give you a good opportunity to analyse paragraph structures.

The functions and structures of paragraphs

The way you structure a paragraph should be informed by the function of the paragraph. This function will largely be determined by how you want the paragraph to help you to respond to the essay question, and should also be influenced by the ever-present requirements that your essays demonstrate knowledge and critical thinking. This advice, however, is quite general. To understand what you can do in individual paragraphs, we need to return to the discussion of task words in Chapter 6.

There we identified three question types: questions which ask you to demonstrate knowledge, questions which ask you to explore complexity and questions which ask you to make evaluations and present your own original perspectives. Paragraphs themselves are involved in these same three activities, and quite often, individual paragraphs will do all three. For example, even an ostensibly straightforward task such as defining a term can involve exploring and evaluating a range of competing definitions and making your own modifications.

Box 10.1 introduces some common functions of paragraphs and their corresponding structures. You will notice the three activities just mentioned arising again and again. Note that the paragraph structures described are simplified; as you will see in the examples in this chapter, actual paragraphs often combine functions or repeat structural elements.

Box 10.1   Some basic paragraph functions and their corresponding structures

Function	Structure (Note that for each structure it is possible to include concluding sentences which link the discussion in the paragraph with the question, the essay's thesis or later discussions.)
Demonstrating what is known (about, for example, an event, or a social or physical phenomenon)	Topic sentence(s) makes a general claim about what is known. Subsequent sentences provide details and possibly reasoning and evidence. If conflicting perspectives exist, the nature of the conflict should be clarified and an evaluation should follow explaining which perspective is preferred.
Showing a relation of cause and effect	Topic sentence(s) identifies a phenomenon. Subsequent sentences explain the cause or effect of this phenomenon. If conflicting perspectives exist, the nature of the conflict should be clarified and an evaluation should follow explaining which perspective is preferred.
Defining a term or explaining a concept or theory	Topic sentence(s) introduces the term, concept or theory. Subsequent sentences provide details. If conflicting perspectives exist, the nature of the conflict should be clarified and an evaluation should follow explaining which perspective is preferred.
Comparing/ contrasting perspectives or phenomena	Topic sentence(s) introduces the idea that two perspectives or phenomena are similar or different. Subsequent sentences provide details of the similarities or differences.
Evaluating a claim or practice	Topic sentence(s) introduces the claim or practice. Subsequent sentences provide details and use reasoning and evidence to establish the true/not true aspects of the claim or the good/bad aspects of the practice.
Making a claim	Topic sentence(s) introduces the claim. Subsequent sentences provide details and substantiate the claim with reasoning and evidence. Counter perspectives are sometimes considered and dismissed.

Analysis of paragraph structures

The structures of three paragraphs will now be analysed. For each, the function of the paragraph in relation to the broader essay will be considered, as well as how this function affects the paragraph's structure. How the paragraph helps to demonstrate knowledge and critical thinking will also be identified.

From an essay about the limited liability company

The first paragraph (Example 10.1) is drawn from an essay from a course on Corporate Law. The essay question, which we saw in Activity 8.1, was, 'In what circumstances is the judiciary prepared to relax the doctrine of the separate legal personality of a company? Is the current legal situation satisfactory from a policy point of view, particularly in the light of the group structure of many modern businesses?' This question may sound confusing if you are unfamiliar with the area, but the problem it is addressing is straightforward. Companies have limited liability, meaning

Example 10.1 An 'evaluating a practice' paragraph

[1] Part of the commercial reality today is that corporate groups are using the principle established in Salomon to their advantage by limiting liability to subsidiary companies (Moore 2006:181). [2] By establishing subsidiary companies in foreign countries to undertake profitable but risky operations, the parent reaps the rewards if the subsidiary turns out to be successful. [3] However, if the subsidiary fails and incurs a hefty liability, then a strict application would limit liability to the subsidiary and the rest of the corporate group would remain unaffected. [4] This results in serious injustice if the subsidiary is severely undercapitalized while undertaking ultra-hazardous operations in developing countries. [5] Clearly, this is an important issue that deserves further scrutiny.

Analysis

- [1] The practice of limiting liability to subsidiary companies is introduced.
- [2] Benefit 1 of practice.
- [3] Benefit 2 of practice.
- [4] Drawback 1 of practice. Note how the words 'serious', 'severely' and 'ultra-hazardous' imply a strong negative critique.
- [5] Concluding sentence affirms the significance of the problem and indicates that more detailed discussions will follow.

that if a company fails its debts are not transferred to its shareholders. This encourages risk taking, which has both benefits and drawbacks.

Paragraph function: evaluating a practice

Paragraph structure: practice introduced, benefit 1, benefit 2, drawback 1, concluding sentence

The paragraph comes from early in the body of the essay, just after the essay has explained the key concepts and legal principles relevant to the question. The paragraph performs the necessary function of clarifying the main problem with the group structure of many modern businesses (see the essay question). Given that the function of the paragraph is to clarify the nature of a problem, it makes sense that the paragraph adopts an 'evaluating a practice' structure. Its topic sentence introduces the general function of the group structure. The subsequent sentences outline the benefits and drawbacks of the group structure and include evaluations that establish the significance of the subject. From this synopsis we can see that the paragraph demonstrates knowledge, explores complexity and makes evaluations. All of the evaluative elements make the student's voice strong.

From an essay about the possibility of conducting humanitarian interventions on environmental grounds

The next two paragraphs come from an essay from a course on International Environmental Law. The essay question was, 'Is there a case for humanitarian intervention on environmental grounds? What legal and other problems might be encountered?' In recent decades there has been a growing, albeit still somewhat weak, international consensus that it is permissible for a state or collection of states to violate the sovereignty and intervene in the affairs of another state to prevent serious crimes such as genocide. Given that environmental degradation has the potential to affect a great many lives, it is worth considering whether current laws and norms regarding humanitarian intervention could be relevant to environmental matters. Example 10.2 contains the skeleton of the essay. The essay adopts the logical structure of first establishing the current state of environmental law, before considering environmental law in relation to human rights and then in relation to humanitarian intervention in particular.

A paragraph from Section 1

(Example 10.3)

Paragraph function: demonstrating what is known/making a claim

Paragraph structure: event introduced, details provided, claim made, details and evidence provided

Example 10.2   Skeleton of the essay

Essay question
Is there a case for humanitarian intervention on environmental grounds? What legal and other problems might be encountered?

Thesis
This essay argues that it is useful to frame environmental issues with respect to their impact on human rights, and that, once this is done, a case for humanitarian interventions on environmental grounds can be made. However, many serious practical concerns remain about whether such interventions would be appropriate or even possible.

Section 1 The current state of domestic and international environmental law

Section 2 The benefits of taking a human rights approach to environmental protection

Section 3 Environmental protection in relation to current laws on humanitarian intervention
3a: Clarifying the current laws on humanitarian intervention (the Responsibility to Protect)
3b: Linking environmental degradation with the Responsibility to Protect

Section 4 Problems with humanitarian intervention on environmental grounds

The first section of the essay has two functions. First, it clarifies recent developments in environmental law. By doing this knowledge is demonstrated. However, this section also prepares the way for later sections when environmental law is considered in the context of human rights law. It does this by making the claim that environmental laws are frequently 'soft' or ineffective, the point being that they would benefit from being linked with more effective human rights legislation. By identifying this pattern the student is demonstrating critical thinking. The individual paragraphs in this section very much reflect these two functions. Example 10.3 contains one of these 'hybrid' paragraphs.

A paragraph from Section 2

(Example 10.4)

Paragraph function: making a claim

Paragraph structure: claim introduced and details provided, example provided, counterpoint introduced, counterpoint partially dismissed

Section 2 makes the claim that at an international level it is useful to pursue concerns about the environment through human rights law. Given this

Example 10.3   A 'demonstrating what is known'/'making a claim' paragraph

[1] The 1992 United Nations Conference on Environment and Development, held in Rio de Janeiro (Rio Conference), firmly announced that environmental issues were a major issue on the international agenda. [2] It was attended by 176 States and saw the release of more soft law declarations, such as the 'Rio Declaration' and the action plan 'Agenda 21' which was adopted by all 176 states in attendance. [3] One of the most important issues that gained international recognition at the Rio Conference is the Precautionary Principle which was outlined in Principle 15 of the Rio Declaration on Environment and Development (Rio Declaration). [4] It states: 'In order to protect the environment, the precautionary approach shall be widely applied by States according to their capabilities. [5] Where there are threats of serious or irreversible damage, lack of scientific certainty shall not be used as a reason for postponing cost-effective measures to prevent environmental degradation' (Hunter, Salzman & Zaeleke 2007, p. 510). [6] However, this is another clear example of a soft law statement of intent that has been largely ignored by the international community. [7] Economic and trade concerns consistently trump the Precautionary Principle, in part due to the soft law nature of the Rio Declaration but also due to the hard law ramifications of trade law such as World Trade Organisation (WTO) rules. [8] WTO Rules are of particular note as they directly contradict the Precautionary Principle requiring scientific certainty before a state may exercise its authority to prevent industry from employing practices that will be detrimental to the environment. [9] The fact that WTO rules contain strong penalties which are consistently enforced does much to preclude states' adherence to the soft law of the Precautionary Principle (Majone 2002, p. 90).

Analysis

- [1]–[5] First broad and then more detailed knowledge of the 1992 Conference is presented. The words 'firmly announced' and 'One of the most important issues' give the impression that the student has a good understanding of the subject.
- [6] The claim is made that the Precautionary Principle is another instance in a pattern of ineffective environmental legislation.
- [7]–[9] Details and evidence are provided for why the Precautionary Principle has been ineffective.

purpose, it makes sense that the individual paragraphs within this section make a series of claims about why this is the case. Example 10.4 contains one of these paragraphs. Not only does the paragraph help the student develop their argument, it gives them an opportunity to continue to demonstrate knowledge about international environmental and human rights law. Critical thinking is demonstrated by the student's introduction and negotiation of a possible counterpoint.

Example 10.4   A 'making a claim' paragraph

[1] Another clear strength of framing arguments for environmental protection through human rights is that, as has already been examined, international environmental law is composed almost exclusively of soft law that is consistently ignored by the international community, particularly the world's largest polluters. [2] Human rights law, on the other hand, is considerably more developed. [3] There are a wide range of treaties and instruments that are clearly binding on states and have repercussions attached to them. [4] Many of these instruments have further crystallised into customary international law through clear *opinio juris* and many decades of state practice. [5] By utilising human rights law for environmental protection purposes it may be possible to circumvent the soft law aspects of international environmental law in favour of the binding commitments outlined in human rights treaties. [6] This is particularly relevant for victims of environmental disasters. [7] As Abate explains: 'human rights approaches [as opposed to environmental approaches] offer quasi-judicial procedures and allow injured parties to appeal to an international body for redress. [8] This process helps protect individuals and communities who would otherwise have very limited legal and political recourse' (Abate 2007, p.20). [9] It could be argued that it will still be hard to achieve binding judgements through human rights channels. [10] However, Koivurova makes the important point that cases brought under human rights law, and the non-binding judgements that may eventuate, nonetheless publicly highlight the plight of those affected by climate change, giving them a louder voice globally and adding to the ever increasing array of arguments with which to attack the practices of the world's biggest polluters (Koivurova 2007 p.298). [11] Thus even unsuccessful cases provide important political gains.

Analysis

- [1]–[2] Claim introduced; namely it is beneficial to frame arguments for environmental protection using human rights law because the latter is considerably more developed.
- [3]–[5] Details are provided clarifying why the approach is beneficial.
- [6]–[8] An example is provided.
- [9] A counterpoint is introduced.
- [10]–[11] The counterpoint is partially dismissed.

Conclusion

This chapter has introduced a number of paragraph functions. While paragraphs can do many things, it is hopefully clear that regardless of the function, much of the time, similar activities happen within them. Most paragraphs begin by making some sort of claim. The body of the paragraph then provides details, and where relevant, gives reasoning and evidence to support the claim and presents counter perspectives. As has been shown, what occurs in a paragraph should derive from how the paragraph helps to answer the essay question.

Essay Conclusions

Introduction

Students are sometimes confused about conclusions. They are often told that conclusions should summarise what has been achieved in the essay. However, on the one hand, they encounter academic articles and books whose conclusions keep arguing rather than summarising. And on the other hand, they worry that if their conclusions only include a summary they will be repetitive. Both of these concerns are well founded. Nevertheless, there is a good way to go about writing conclusions and it need not be overly repetitive. Although conclusions and introductions include similar information, they emphasise different things. Introductions are concerned with introducing the question/problem to be addressed and explaining its significance, and giving a brief overview of what will be covered. Conclusions are more concerned with summarising the key arguments that have been made; this summary will be more substantial than the outline in the introduction.

This chapter will begin by saying a little more about why conclusions exist; this will involve some reflections on the form of the essay itself. After this it will clarify what should and should not appear in conclusions and discuss the language you can use.

Why conclusions? Comparing essays with reports of empirical research

To better understand essay conclusions it is useful to compare essays with reports of empirical research. These reports are common, occurring in the sciences, social sciences, business and other disciplines. An important difference between essays and these reports is that the report structure reflects a problem solving process, whereas the essay structure tends not to (this point was touched on in Chapter 8 when discussing theses).

The typical sections in a report of empirical research are: introduction, method, results, discussion and conclusion. These reflect the process of first identifying a problem, then coming up with a method to solve it, then collecting data using this method, and then analysing the data and drawing conclusions. Given this, it makes sense that we do not learn about the solution to the problem until the conclusion.

Now, even though essays are concerned with solving problems, they do not involve conducting empirical research. Rather, the writer of an essay arrives at a conclusion following a period of reading, thinking and writing. *The finished essay presents the outcome of this process, not the process itself;* the process is 'messy' and there is no point trying to reflect it in the essay's structure.

Given this, it is common for an essay's conclusion to be presented in the introduction. This is the essay's thesis or general argument. When this occurs, the actual conclusion functions as a reminder of what was achieved in the body of the essay.

What should appear in a conclusion?

As we saw in Chapter 8, a number of different elements can appear in an introduction. For example, the orientation alone needs to introduce the subject, explain why the subject is significant, perhaps point out key tensions and debates, perhaps define key terms, introduce the problem to be addressed and indicate why the problem is significant. Conclusions are more straightforward. Box 11.1 outlines a standard way to structure a conclusion.

Box 11.1   The structure of a conclusion

Stage in conclusion	Explanation
Brief reminder of question/ problem being addressed	Consider spending a sentence or two orienting the conclusion by reminding the reader about the question/problem being addressed by the essay.
Summary of main points	Spend the bulk of the conclusion summarising the main arguments made in the body of the essay in the order they were made. Take care to show the relations between the points. This summary is often more detailed than the outline in the introduction.
(Re)statement of thesis	If the question requires it, finish by restating your thesis. Or, if you did not include a thesis in your introduction, state your general response.

What should not appear in a conclusion?

New information

A common preference of markers is that new information is not included in conclusions. Therefore, do not keep building your arguments. However, consistent with what has been said, it is acceptable, if you have not articulated a thesis in your introduction, to tie together all of the points you have made in the body of your essay with a general statement that answers the question.

Mismatched general arguments

Thinking about the writing process and its 'messiness', you will sometimes find that you will start writing your essay not being certain about what you are arguing, but once you get to the end your position becomes clear. Trailing clouds of glory you type out your general argument in your conclusion and then submit your essay. The problem is that this general argument, because it is the last thing you thought of, is often inconsistent with the earlier parts of your essay. The simple point is that if you do write yourself into clarity, you need to go back through your essay and ensure that all of your arguments are consistent.

Unimportant information

When students are told they need to summarise what they have said in the body, they often think they need to outline the entire structure of the essay. This is not necessary, and doing so can cause a conclusion to sound wooden. The summary should focus on the *important arguments* that were advanced in the body – the arguments that ultimately lead to the question being answered. The conclusion in Example 11.1 comes from an Abnormal Psychology essay (we have seen extracts from this essay earlier). It is little more than a structural outline and thus is painfully wooden. Note that it hardly extends beyond the question, giving no sense of the original work done in the essay.

Banal final sentences

Finally, it seems to be some kind of hangover from early high school assignments that students like to finish their essays with a horrible banality. Finish your essays with a strong general point. Do not degrade them by writing something like, 'But what the future holds, no one can say'; or 'But this is just one perspective. There are many others'; or 'Maybe the world will never be perfect, but we can at least try to make it better.'

Example 11.1   A conclusion that achieves little

Essay question

Examine the case of "Isabella", a woman who has been diagnosed with Adjustment Disorder with Anxiety, and prescribed Mindfulness-Based Stress Reduction. Evaluate her diagnosis and prescribed treatment. If appropriate, suggest a new diagnosis and treatment.

Conclusion

[1] This essay has analysed the case of "Isabella", a woman who had been diagnosed with Adjustment Disorder with Anxiety, and prescribed Mindfulness-Based Stress Reduction. [2] First, the essential details of Isabella's case were examined. [3] Second, her diagnosis and prescription were evaluated. [4] A new diagnosis was proposed and justified. [5] Lastly, several treatment options including the originally prescribed Mindfulness-Based Stress Reduction were discussed.

Analysis

- [1] This sentence is acceptable because it reminds the reader of what the essay was about. However, it might have been better to frame this first sentence as a problem, that is, say something about there being possible inaccuracies in Isabella's diagnosis and prescribed treatment.
- [2] There is no need to mention this at all. The conclusion should move straight to discussing Isabella's diagnosis and prescription.
- [3] More details should be included here: the nature of the evaluation should be mentioned.
- [4] The new diagnosis and its justification should be specified.
- [5] Once again, more details are needed. This sentence tells us nothing.

What language should be used in conclusions? Tense and signposting

When summarising the actual information you presented and the arguments you made in the body of the essay, you should stick to the present tense. However, it can be useful to incorporate signposting that employs the past simple (for example, 'This essay *argued* that …') or present perfect tenses (for example, 'This essay *has argued* that …'; 'This essay *has analysed* the case of …', 'We *have examined* …'). Using such signposting makes it clear that you are looking back to what occurred in the body of the essay and can also help to lead your reader through your arguments (for example, 'First, it was demonstrated that …'; 'Second, X and Y were examined …'; 'It was proposed that …'; 'We also saw that …').

Present tense signposting can also be used (for example, 'Taken together, these three points lead us to conclude that ...'). While signposting is not essential, it can help to prevent your conclusions from becoming bullet point-like summaries of the body of your essay. For weaker essays which do not employ any signposting, and which also introduce new information, it can be very hard to tell that the conclusion is a conclusion.

Finally, there is the question of whether you should begin your conclusion with the words 'In conclusion' or 'To conclude' or something similar. Some markers do not like this because they believe it sounds clichéd, and also because the language you use should make it obvious that your conclusion is your conclusion. However, as I have at times suggested, if you are unsure, put clarity before stylistic concerns and write 'In conclusion'.

For an example of a strong conclusion, see the second sample essay in the next chapter. You will probably need to read the full essay to understand why the conclusion is strong.

Improve the conclusion   ACTIVITY 11.1

The conclusion in this activity comes from the essay we studied in Chapter 10 about the possibility of conducting humanitarian interventions on environmental grounds. Look back over the skeleton if you need to refamiliarise yourself with the essay. The conclusion summarises the key points of the essay. However, it reads a bit like a series of bullet points, and a definitive response to the question is missing. Drawing on what has been discussed in this chapter, write an improved version of the conclusion. Some thoughts are provided in the Appendix.

Essay question
Is there a case for humanitarian intervention on environmental grounds? What legal and other problems might be encountered?

Conclusion
There is a clear link between the violation of human rights and environmental degradation. The 'harder' law of human rights instruments can give legal strength to environmental concerns when they are framed in a human rights perspective. It is also possible to identify a link between the human rights violated by environmental degradation and the crimes of genocide and crimes against humanity. However, this link is highly debatable and would certainly be challenged. Should this link be accepted, there is an argument that humanitarian intervention to prevent environmental degradation would be justified under the Responsibility to Protect doctrine, which is slowly moving towards acceptance as a norm of international law. However, problems abound, not least of which is the fact that the world's biggest polluters, who would be the natural targets of any intervention, also control the world's strongest militaries.

Conclusion

Box 11.2 summaries what has been discussed in this chapter from the perspective of what you should include, perhaps include and not include in your conclusions.

Box 11.2   Things to include, perhaps include and not include in your conclusions

Do
Summarise the main arguments made in the body.
Restate your thesis, or if you did not state a thesis in your introduction and the question invites it, state your general response to the question.
Ensure the thesis in your conclusion is consistent with the arguments in the body and, if relevant, with the thesis in your introduction.
Optional
Orient your conclusion by reiterating the question/problem being addressed.
Write 'In conclusion'.
Use past simple or present perfect tense to make your conclusion sound like a conclusion.
Do not
Include new information.
Waste words summarising inconsequential points.
Summarise your points in a different order compared with the body.
Finish your conclusion with a banal statement.

12

Analysing Complete Essays

Introduction

I conclude this book by analysing two complete essays: a weaker and a stronger one. The essays were chosen because they are accessible and illustrate much of what has been covered, and also because they are relatively short. Comments are made throughout. Most transition signals and reporting verbs and phrases have been underlined, and occasionally extraneous words have been struck out. After each essay, comments are made on a marking sheet whose criteria closely follow the topics covered in the book.

A weaker essay

Our first complete essay comes from a course which explored comedy. The 1350 word essay was responding to the question, 'Why do we like to laugh?' As there are many theories across the sciences and arts about why we like to laugh, the question very much lends itself to the three basic academic activities of showing knowledge, exploring complexity and making evaluations. The essay is weak because it is poorly structured and dominated by others' ideas (the student's voice is not sufficiently present). Also, while much of what it discusses is broadly relevant, the student often does not clearly link their points with the question.

Essay question
Why do we like to laugh?

Essay 1
Fundamentally we like to laugh because it makes us feel good.
The explanations, however, for why laughter makes us feel

This first sentence might look like a thesis; however it is not really. Insofar as liking something and feeling good about something are the same thing, the argument is circular.

good are complex and come from many different~~~ disciplines. ~~In order~~ to address this question it is first ~~of all~~ necessary to ~~briefly~~ discuss what laughter is and why we laugh ~~at all~~, and then the discussion will ~~go on to~~ consider the benefits of laughter and why we like to laugh.

> If this second sentence were rephrased it would be the basis for a good orientation. This is because it is a broad statement which acknowledges that the subject is complex.

> It would have been best to stick to the question: no need to add 'the benefits of laughter'.

> This last sentence is the essay's outline. However, there is too much repetition. For example, 'why we laugh' is very close to 'why we like to laugh'.

Laughter can be understood as "the most common expression of humorous experience" which involves a particular form of vocal expression and a respiratory pattern (Provine et al, cited in Martin, 2001 p. 505). Not all humour is responded to with laughter, and not all laughter is in response to humour, however laughter is a very common physical way in which people respond to comedy or humour or express humour. (Martin, 2001 p505).

> While this first sentence is clearly responding to the question, 'What is laughter?' (thus it fits with the outline in the introduction), the student's voice is nonetheless diminished because the sentence is a mixture of quotation and paraphrase.

> Punctuation should come after the citation.

> This is inconsistent. Earlier 'p.' was used.

Laughter is more than just a vocal sound and has been referred to as a language (O'Shannon, 2012). Anthropologists <u>explain</u> that laughter is a form of communication and a universal language with laughter being one of the first kinds of vocalisations that babies make between the ages of two to six months (Darwin 1872 cited in Gervais & Wilson, 2005, p397). This suggests that the capacity to laugh is innate and is part of our evolution as human beings. Bergson <u>argues</u> that humour and laughter are unique to humans and that this ability is because we have the ability for higher-ordered thinking (~~seen in~~ H, D & A, 2011). Laughter has been explained as having an "adaptive function" and is hypothesised as originally being "a signal of safety to the group, an expression of unity in group opinion prior to language" (H, D & A, 2011 p38). Humour and laughter seem to be a universal characteristic of the human species and common to all cultures, although can be expressed and experienced differently (Weisfeld, 1993).

> This paragraph is a paragraph fragment; it should be longer. Also, the student's voice is barely present.

> This is a new paragraph; however, in part it is responding to the same question as the previous paragraph ('What is laughter?'). A structural rethink was needed. Also, this paraphrase in the topic sentence further diminishes the student's voice.

> Confusing citation. Was Darwin the one talking about the anthropologists? Seems unlikely. Thus it is not obvious where the information in the first part of the sentence came from.

> Clumsy referent.

> Names should be used.

> This is repetitive. The same point was made in the third sentence of the paragraph.

> Like the previous paragraph and later paragraphs, this paragraph is a patchwork of others' ideas (it is a 'plagiphrase' paragraph).

(Continued)

According to Martin (2001) the benefits of laughter have been well accepted even since biblical times. Physicians and philosophers have noted that "laughter benefits health through a variety of mechanisms, including providing physical exercise to the muscles, lungs and inner organs of the body, enriching the blood, increasing respiration and blood circulation, improving digestion, and providing emotional catharsis" (p504). While these benefits of laughter are accepted as common wisdom, there have been some more recent studies that refute this idea amongst some sections of the population. For example, one study that examined the psychological and physical benefits of laughter for patients with chronic obstructive pulmonary disease, found that in spite of the benefits of a positive attitude and sense of humour on the overall wellbeing of the patient, the physical act of laughing had a negative impact on them physiologically as it resulted in poorer pulmonary functioning (Lebowitz et al, 2011). So although it is accepted that we like to laugh, there are certain circumstances where some people may not enjoy the act of laughing as it has a negative impact on their health.

There is growing evidence that laughter can stimulate the immune system by boosting the body's production of interferon, which fights viruses and reduces stress hormones (Martin, 2001). Scott et al (2014) suggest that laughter is more than just a positive emotional expression but that it is associated with improved physiological responses to stress and negative emotions. It is perhaps this reason that we like to laugh as it has an inbuilt physiological reward for us in dealing with negative emotions and negative thoughts. Laughter has a positive impact on our mood and can even influence our response to or our perception of pain (Ayan, 2009). It has been

---

The student's voice is again weak in this topic sentence. Also, are we to assume that the benefits of laughter are the reasons why we like to laugh? It is important to stick to the language of the question. Also, this topic sentence is too broad – the essay could have begun with it.

It is good that the student is introducing a counterpoint; however, this counterpoint is not really relevant. See next comment.

This is a concluding sentence; however, it seems to be responding to the question, 'Is laughter always enjoyable?'

Structurally this paragraph is an improvement on the previous one. Also, the student's voice is stronger.

Once again the student's voice is weak in the topic sentence.

This is better. The student is linking what they have been arguing with the question. However, perhaps this sentence would have worked better at the end of the paragraph. Also, the paragraph has moved on from the discussion of the immune system introduced in the topic sentence. The rule of one point per paragraph is broken.

This sentence overlaps with the second sentence of the paragraph. It feels out of place coming after the previous sentence.

shown that married couples who are very satisfied in their relationship use laughter as an effective coping strategy in dealing with problems or negativity (Martin, 2001).

Hurley et al (2011) suggest that release theories of humour support the idea that laughter has a role in dealing with tension. They argue that when nervous energy builds up, it needs to be released. When this occurs through the release of positive emotion, the tension is converted to laughter. This idea of the benefit laughter has in releasing tension was supported by Freud, whether for the individual or in a tense social situation when humour and laughter is used to 'break the ice' (O'Shannon, 2012). For people who are anxious or tense, laughing at a joke can have the effect of easing that anxiety, whether it is because it distances the person from the anxiety and negative thoughts or whether it changes the person physiologically (Ayan, 2009).

It is important however to differentiate between humour and laughing when considering the benefits. Many humour researchers argue that the real physical and psychological benefits result from the psychology of humour more than laughter itself (Ayan, 2009). Having a sense of humour is clearly related to the predisposition to be able to laugh, however there needs to be a distinction between the benefits of having a sense of humour, which may be more of a personality trait, and the benefits of laughter, which is particularly involved with the physical act of laughing. For example a person may have a negative disposition and not be very optimistic, and yet they may still enjoy laughing and experiencing the physical benefits of laughter.

> An improved topic sentence would have been, 'A third reason we like to laugh is because it helps us manage tension.' Perhaps the point about married couples could have been included as part of this point.

> This is repetitive. Instead of building this paragraph out of paraphrases, given their similar content, the paraphrases could have been summarised.

> The student's voice is strong in this topic sentence. The problem, however, is that it is not obvious that this discussion, which seems tangential, will help to answer the question. This concern is born out in the paragraph.

(Continued)

This could be because there are many social reasons why people laugh and like to laugh.

> This concluding sentence attempts to make the content of the paragraph relevant to the question, but it does not quite succeed because it is too general.

Researchers have found that the majority of laughter takes place within conversations between people. Although it is possible to laugh at something while on your own, it is most common to be in a social situation with one or more people while laughing takes place. As Scott says

> Who are these researchers? A citation is needed. Also, a better topic sentence was possible. For example, 'We like to laugh because laughter performs an important social function'.

> Informal.

"laughter is mediated strongly by social context: we are 30-fold more likely to laugh if we are with someone else than if we are on our own" (Scott, 2014 p.618). Laughter is predominantly a

> This overlaps heavily with the previous sentence. Once again, instead of stacking up paraphrases – or in this case quotations and paraphrases – a summary could have been used to combine the information.

relational act, and involves either making others laugh, which is known to be an attractive feature (Martin, 2001), or to laugh in response to

> The grammar goes wrong here.

something or someone.

> On the positive side, this paragraph sticks to one main point.

One study found that there were therapeutic benefits for dementia sufferers, not only in laughing in a passive sense, but also in being active participants in creating comedy and making others laugh (Stevens, 2011). Although there needs to be more research in this area, it seems that even having dementia did not stop the elderly people in the study from getting enjoyment from laughing (Stevens, 2011).

> This example could have been integrated into the previous paragraph.

> Relevance of point not clear.

> This paragraph is another paragraph fragment.

Laughter can also be used for less admirable reasons such as suggested by Superiority Theory (H, D & A, 2011). According to this theory, laughter can be in response to others' misfortune or "laughing, especially in social situations, typically does imply membership in an elite group" (H, D & A, 2011 p.41). The comedian Stephen Fry has observed that humour is culturally determined.

> More needed to be done to link this topic sentence with the question. For example, 'We also like to laugh because doing so can be an expression of superiority.'

> The quotation is not well integrated into the sentence.

> There is too much of a jump between the previous sentence and this one. The rule of one point per paragraph is in danger of being broken.

In America people laugh at situations that involve someone making fun of another who is less privileged or less successful, while in the UK it is the opposite. This <u>suggests</u> that <u>although</u> the capacity to laugh is universal, the motivation for laughing and why we like to laugh may be more determined by the context and culture.

> The focus has now clearly shifted to making cultural comparisons.

> This is a good point; however, it deserves its own paragraph. There is a disjunction between the concluding sentence and the topic sentence.

    People like to use laughter as a way of breaking down awkward social situations. As Gervais and Wilson describe it, laughter often "facilitates friendliness" (2005 p400).

> This is a stronger topic sentence. The student's voice is clear and the question is being addressed. However, this point has already been covered in the earlier discussion of relief theory.

The laughter that takes place even amongst strangers listening to a stand-up comedian can bring people together and give them a sense of oneness in the shared activity of laughter. Laughter is a social activity that is also about amusement, entertainment and relaxation and has a contagious feature (Scott, 2014) so that we can laugh at each other laughing, without necessarily knowing why.

> This is a separate point from the topic sentence and it too has already been covered.

> This paragraph is another paragraph fragment.

    There are many physical and psychological benefits of laughter and growing scientific evidence to account for how this occurs. The reason we laugh seems to be a unique feature of being human beings and the way we have evolved. However why we like to laugh seems to be more connected to the social nature of humans and our need for interaction and experiencing pleasure with each other.

> Better to use the language of the question and write 'why'.

> This reason is not sufficiently specific.

> The transition signal 'However' does not work. What follows does not contradict what has just been said.

> The student concludes with a general argument that goes some way to answering the question. It partially incorporates the arguments made in the body of the essay: the body did often discuss the social function of laughter.

(Continued)

References

Ayan S, (2009). 'Laughing Matters', *Scientific American Mind*, pp. 24–31.

Grevais M, and Wilson D, (2005). 'The Evolution and Functions of Laughter and Humour: A Synthetic Approach', The Quarterly Review of Biology, Vol. 80, No. 4, pp. 395–430.

Hurley M, Dennett D, & Adams R, (2011). *A Breif History of Humour Therioes, Chapter 4, Inside Jokes: Using Humour to Reverse-Engineer the Mind*, Massachusetts and London: the MIT Press, p37–54

Lebowitz KR, et al, (2011). 'Effects of humour and laughter on psychological...' Heart & Lung, Department of Psychology, Ohio State University, Columbus, OH

Martin R, (2001). '*Humour, Laughter, and Physical Health, Methodological Issues and Research Findings*', Psychological Bulletin, American Psychological Association Vol. 127 No. 4, p504–519.

O'Shannon D, (2012). *What Are You Lauging At?*: A Comprehensive Guide to the Comedic Event, New York and London: Continuum.

Scott S, et al, 2014. '*The social life of laughter*', Trends in Cognitive Sciences, Vol. 18, p618–620, London UK.

Stevens J, (2011). '*Stand up for Dementia....*', Southern Cross University, SAGE, Australia

Stephen Fry: https://www.youtube.com/watch?v=8k2AbqTBxao Cited: 09/06/2015

Weisfeld GE, (1993). '*The Adaptive Value of Humour and Laughter*', Department of Psychology, Ethology and Sociobiology, Detroit, p141–169

Wilson DW, (1992). '*Why Do We Laugh*', The Scientific Monthly Vol. 15, No. 4 343–347, Published by: American Association for the Advancement of Science, Stable URL: <http://www.jstor.org/stable/6903> Cited: 08/06/2015

Only some corrections are made to the reference list.

Is there a volume or an issue number?

Italics needed for journal title. This is a recurring problem.

Inconsistent. See previous reference.

Should be 'pp'. This is a recurring problem.

Unless there are a large number of authors, present all names in the reference list.

No italics for article title. This is a recurring problem.

Keep going!

Should be 'Fry, S', and listed under 'F' rather than 'S'.

Essay 1 marking sheet

Is the introduction well constructed? • Orientation • Thesis • Outline	The introduction is weak. It begins with the thesis, not an orientation, and the thesis contributes little because it is circular. There is a sentence of orientation after the thesis. This is the best aspect of the introduction. The outline barely moves beyond the level of generality of the question.
Is the body well constructed? • General logic (essay's skeleton) • Structure of individual paragraphs	The body is not well constructed. It is hard to follow the general logic of the essay: there is considerable repetition from one paragraph to the next and clear topic sentences are often lacking. Individual paragraphs regularly break the rules of paragraph construction: it is not always obvious how the material being discussed helps to answer the question; paragraphs are often too short; topic sentences are weak because they are often paraphrases; concluding sentences are mostly absent; the logic within paragraphs is not clear – few transition signals are used; there is often more than one point per paragraph; there is not a good balance between the student's voice and the voices of others.
Is the conclusion well constructed? • Summary • Thesis (re)stated	The conclusion is too brief. There is very little summary. However, the essay does finish with a general argument that partially incorporates the arguments made in the essay.
Is knowledge and understanding of the subject demonstrated?	Insofar as the student has included a lot of relevant information in their essay, we could say that they demonstrate some knowledge of the subject. However, given the student never creates summaries combining multiple sources, rarely considers the similarities and differences between perspectives, nor makes any evaluations, it is hard to say they have understanding.
Are the sources well integrated?	While the information from sources is sometimes introduced and citations are regularly provided, this essay is guilty of what we called 'plagiphrasing'. The student lets others' words replace their own. This is exacerbated by the fact that others' work is rarely analysed. Rather than building their paragraphs by joining paraphrases, the student should have created combined summaries of others' ideas and followed these with analyses.
Is the referencing correct? • In-text referencing • Reference list	While there are some inconsistencies in the in-text citations, the student has for the most part done a reasonable job of acknowledging the sources they use. However, the reference list contains a too many errors. Notably, the student does not always manage to identify journal articles as journal articles.

(*Continued*)

Is critical thinking demonstrated?	While there are moments when the student demonstrates insight, it is hard to identify much critical thinking because for the most part the student's voice is absent. The weak structure also diminishes the impression of critical thinking.
Is there a sustained and convincing engagement with the question?	While much of the material included is relevant to the question, it is rarely used by the student to explicitly answer the question; thus there is not a sustained and convincing engagement with the question.
Is the expression appropriate? • Level of formality • Grammar	As the student's voice is absent for most of the essay, it is hard to say whether the expression is appropriate. When the student's voice is present, the level of formality seems reasonable. There are some grammatical errors.
General comment	This essay is not really an essay. The student has found a lot of useful material, but this material has not been presented in an orderly way. Instead, quotations and paraphrases have been joined together in a somewhat haphazard manner. For this to become an essay, a good first step would be to come up with a clear essay skeleton. With this in place, strong topic sentences could be developed and the supporting material could begin to be integrated. The main topics to discuss would include the following: (1) laughter's ability to create group unity (in both large groups and in intimate relationships); (2) related to (1), the interesting link between laughter and superiority; (3) also related to (1), laughter's ability to ease tension; (4) the physical benefits of laughter. Perhaps the discussion of what laughter is could be jettisoned.

A stronger essay

Our second complete essay is responding to a question we have now seen on a few occasions, 'To what extent is the quality of a society affected by the quality of its leader(s)?' The 1350-word essay was written as part of an introductory course on Political Philosophy. The question is broad and many different approaches are possible. The essay is impressive for several reasons.

• It is structurally clear and logical: there is a tight relationship between the question, thesis and topic sentences, and the elaboration of points within paragraphs is excellent.
• It sustains an argument throughout.
• It packs many thoughtful points into a limited number of words.
• It demonstrates critical thinking by exploring some of the complexities of the subject, by frequently using clever reasoning and by anticipating

objections to arguments. Also, the student's voice is always present.

- It engages thoughtfully with its sources, making good use of summaries; the summaries demonstrate the student has understood the sources.
- On the negative side, while the student does critique their own arguments, there are no critiques of others' ideas, nor is there much comparing and contrasting of others' perspectives.

Essay question

To what extent is the quality of a society affected by the quality of its leader(s)?

| The significance of the subject is implied. |

| A broader subject is introduced. This provides a context for the question. |

Essay 2

| The significance of the problem is indicated. |

An enduring challenge for all societies is ensuring they are well functioning. Regardless of what we understand to be meant by 'well-functioning', an important consideration is the extent to which leaders are able to affect the quality of their societies. If we can understand this, societies themselves will be better equipped to improve their quality. This essay will argue that despite the prominence of leaders throughout history, the extent to which a society's quality is affected by the quality of its leaders is generally minimal. As will be demonstrated, there are three main obstacles preventing leaders from affecting the quality of their society: first, society shapes its potential leaders, second, society chooses its leaders, and third, the quality of society determines the limit of change its leaders can implement. The exception involves a leader using the authoritarian tendencies of their society to effect specific changes.

| The essay question is introduced as a problem. |

| The significance of the problem is clarified. |

| This is a nice touch that demonstrates self-awareness. That is, the student is indicating they are aware their thesis is counterintuitive. |

| The thesis provides a succinct general response to the question. It is good that the thesis is not black and white. |

| Succinct outline. All points clearly support the thesis and help to answer the question. |

(Continued)

The influence of society on the development of potential leaders is the first obstacle preventing leaders from affecting the quality of their society. Bunge (1997) emphasises the strength of society's influence over the individual in his paper on social mechanisms by stating that "individual action and social environment-or agency and structure-always come together because they generate one another." Since potential leaders are individuals within a society, they themselves would be influenced by their society. However, it could be argued that potential leaders are often stronger of character and thus more able to resist the influence of society, but as Socrates (Plato 1987) indicates, sycophants are drawn to such people, seeking to influence those of great potential in the hopes of future gain. This combined influence from both sycophants and society is difficult for even the strongest character to resist. Thus potential leaders, whether of weak character or strong, are shaped by their society. Since society cannot gain leaders of a quality different to its own, society cannot depend on them to alter its quality in general.

Even if there were potential leaders of different quality to society, those potential leaders would not be chosen as society chooses leaders of the same quality as itself. In the republics that dominate modern politics, societies directly choose their leaders through elections. Because it would be foolish for citizens to choose leaders who want different things from themselves, societies choose leaders who reflect their own qualities. But this is not a phenomenon restricted to modern republics. As we read in Machiavelli's *The Prince* (2007), even in a 16th century feudal society, potential leaders needed to be seen to have the same qualities as their

Clear topic sentence. Note the close relationship between this and the first point in the outline.

Page number needed.

Elements from the previous sentence are paraphrased to create a link between the student's and Bunge's ideas.

It is good that some caution is shown.

An impressive moment. The student anticipates an objection to their argument then proceeds to dismiss it.

Good summary.

The order of sycophants and society should be reversed for consistency's sake.

Concluding sentence links argument with question/thesis.

Another impressive moment. The student links the paragraphs using an 'even if' argument. This type of argument shows self-awareness and flexibility. In essence they are saying, 'I may be wrong, but if I am, I have more arguments to support my position.'

A brief but compelling argument. The student appeals to common knowledge. This works well.

The student once again anticipates a possible objection: that their argument is not strong because it is limited to modern republics.

society lest they be overthrown. Thus the society is still effectively choosing the qualities of its leader. Interestingly, even in the case that leaders are overthrown by a portion of society that wants change, the new leaders often end up upholding earlier qualities. In other words, even when it seems the people are choosing leaders of a different quality, they are not. Marx (1969) illustrates this through the example of the French Revolution of 1848. Despite violently overthrowing their government, the people of France allowed a new regime to grow that was very similar to the old. And even Hegel, who applauded the final result of the French Revolution of 1789, had to concede that the immediate result of the revolution was not the liberation it had sought (Marcuse 1977). If the quality of a society does not change even with the violent replacement of previous leaders, it follows logically that the quality of a society does not depend on its leaders.

Should people of different quality to society somehow become and remain leaders, the quality of a society still limits the changes those leaders can implement. Adhering to virtue is not necessarily easy for a society to do, and if a society does not truly value a difficult virtue, it will fail to follow laws created by leaders to enforce this virtue. An example of this is gender equality. Inequality along gender lines has existed in many societies across all of recorded history. It certainly existed in Ancient Greece, where Plato's idea that women could do the same things as men was radical (Okin 1998). In his works, Plato describes two cities: a best city (in the *Republic*) and a second best city (in the *Laws* – written after the *Republic*). The most significant difference between the two cities from a 21st century

> This sentence provides a good summary.

> This is a subtle point, and perhaps it could have been better made. Nevertheless, it represents a nuanced consideration of the subject. Further, the student supports this point with two excellent examples.

> A useful rephrasing to make the point more relevant to the point introduced in the topic sentence.

> The concluding sentence links the arguments made in the paragraph with the thesis/question.

> Another 'even if' argument is introduced which provides a link with the previous paragraph.

> Good elaboration on the topic sentence.

> An illustration is introduced. Note how in what follows the student keeps their own voice strong even while summarising Okin's arguments.

(Continued)

perspective is the extreme differences in gender equality, with female leaders being equal to male leaders in the best city, and women being mere property in the second best city. In her analysis of these writings, Okin (1998) shows how the quality of the two societies is responsible for this dichotomy. We can interpret the Laws as being a recognition by Plato of the fact that even if the philosopher kings of Plato's *Republic* came to rule, the people themselves would not permit the difficult virtues Plato proposes. If adherence to virtues like gender equality is based solely on what citizens will accept, this indicates that the quality of the leaders is irrelevant in the face of societal qualities.

> The student does an excellent job of linking the summary which has just occurred with the argument introduced in the topic sentence.

> Once again the student efficiently links the argument made in the paragraph with their thesis.

While all the above points indicate that a society's quality does not generally depend on its leaders, the exception is when a leader uses the authoritarian tendencies of their people to alter their society's quality. In all societies there is a class of people who are willing to overlook laws, traditions, and the rights of fellow citizens provided these actions are mandated by the leaders of their society (Altemeyer 1996). The most famous example of this phenomenon is the case of Nazi Germany, where the people of Germany allowed their leaders to drastically change the quality of their society. The change was so dramatic that it prompted intense study into the cause, and researchers concluded that the Nazis were able to enact their changes by appealing to people with authoritarian tendencies within their society (Reich 1946). Now this would seem a fairly broad case as these people are present in every society, but they will only support changes that increase the authority of their leaders and with it their own authority over others (Altemeyer 1996). Thus it is only possible for

> The previous arguments are summarised before a counterpoint is introduced.

> A useful example is introduced.

> Note how no transition signal is needed here because the subject of this sentence clearly links with an aspect of the previous sentence.

> The student is a little disingenuous here. They only cite one researcher: Reich.

> Once again the student anticipates an objection to their argument. Two thoughtful points are then introduced to reduce the scope of the objection.

leaders to alter a society's quality through this exception by increasing the power and extent of the law, punishment of criminals, foreign relations aggression, and persecution of minorities. Any change beyond these would encounter the same obstacles as the general case. It should <u>also</u> be noted that presumably those without authoritarian tendencies would resist these changes. <u>Hence,</u> while an exception does exist, it is a very specific exception with narrow applications.

> Concluding sentence clarifies how the counterpoint sits in relation to their broader argument.

   <u>While</u> the notion that leaders are able to affect the quality of societies has intuitive appeal, it is difficult in practice for them to do so. <u>As was argued</u>, potential leaders are influenced by their society to take on society's qualities such that even the strongest potential leaders will be shaped by this influence. <u>And even</u> if potential leaders resist being shaped by their society, the society will still choose only those leaders with the same quality as itself, and will go so far as to overthrow leaders if they do not have that quality. Even following revolutions whose aim is to install leaders who could radically alter the quality of their society, the new leaders end up upholding the earlier societal qualities. <u>Finally</u>, in the unlikely event that leaders of different quality both exist and are allowed to rule, they must still overcome society's innate resistance to change. <u>Against all these obstacles</u> is the ability for leaders to alter a society's quality by using the authoritarian tendencies of its citizens. <u>However, since</u> this is both limited to specific changes, and relies on these people outnumbering or overpowering those without authoritarian tendencies, it is too narrow to be more than a small consideration. With all the obstacles preventing leaders from altering the quality of a society, and with so narrow an exception, <u>it must be concluded that</u> the quality of a society is only affected by the quality of its leader(s) to a minimal extent.

> The conclusion begins with a brief orientation which is a more general version of the student's thesis. This generality is fine here as the thesis is clearly restated at the end of the conclusion.

> Note the use of past tense. This makes it clear that we have entered the conclusion.

> In the following sentences the points from the strong side of the argument are summarised. Care is taken to link them together. Note that this summary is more detailed than the outline in the introduction.

> The point from the weak side of the argument is summarised; the student emphasises the weakness of the argument.

> The conclusion finishes by restating the essay's thesis.

(Continued)

References

Altemeyer, B 1996, *The authoritarian specter*, Harvard University Press, Cambridge, United States.

Bunge, M 1997, 'Mechanism and explanation', *Philosophy of the Social Sciences*, vol. 27, no. 4, pp. 410–465.

Machiavelli, N 2007, *The Prince*, Cambridge University Press, Cambridge, United Kingdom.

Marcuse, H 1977, *Reason and revolution: Hegel and the rise of social theory*, Routledge & Kegan Paul Limited, London, England.

Marx, K 1969, *The eighteenth brumaire of Louis Bonaparte*, International Publishers, New York, United States of America.

Okin, SM 1998, 'Philosopher queens and private wives: plato on women and family', in ND Smith (ed.), *Plato, critical assessments*, Routledge, London, England, pp. 174–193.

Plato 1987, *Plato, the republic*, Penguin Books, England.

Reich, W 1946, *The mass psychology of fascism*, Orgone Institute Press, New York, United States.

Essay 2 marking sheet

Is the introduction well constructed? • Orientation • Thesis • Outline	The introduction is well constructed. The question/problem is introduced in the orientation, there is a clear thesis which answers the question and the points in the outline obviously support the thesis.
Is the body well constructed? • General logic (essay's skeleton) • Structure of individual paragraphs	There is a logical and clear general structure. Paragraphs are well linked. Individual paragraphs are all well organised. Topic and concluding sentences are well executed. Potential counterpoints are artfully integrated.
Is the conclusion well constructed? • Summary • Thesis restated	The conclusion contains a thorough summary which clearly shows how the student developed their argument. Thesis is restated.
Is knowledge and understanding of the subject demonstrated?	The student demonstrates a good understanding of the sources they employ (they produce convincing summaries and paraphrases of individual sources); however, there is not a strong sense that they are aware of the range of perspectives on the subject nor how these perspectives relate to one another. Thus a broad understanding is lacking. This is only a minor problem given the essay was an undergraduate essay and given the strength of the other aspects.

Are the sources well integrated?	Throughout there is a clear differentiation between the student's voice and the voices of the sources. The significance of all sources in relation to the student's arguments is clear. Analysis could sometimes have been improved.
Is the referencing correct? • In-text referencing • Reference list	Referencing is for the most part correct. More page numbers are needed for in-text citations (for quotations and paraphrases).
Is critical thinking demonstrated?	Strong critical thinking is demonstrated throughout: the student's voice is always present, arguments are well laid out, the nuances of individual points are explored, the anticipation of objections is impressive and individual arguments are made efficiently. A strong sense of independence is generated.
Is there a sustained and convincing engagement with the question?	Every aspect of the essay clearly supports the thesis and ultimately contributes to answering the question. We are never unsure about the relevance of a line of argument.
Is the expression appropriate? • Level of formality • Grammar	The expression is appropriately formal. Its concision is noteworthy. Grammar is excellent.
General comment	This essay does very well in the areas of structure, critical thinking and expression. However, while it does engage thoughtfully with its sources, it does not give the impression that the student has a broad understanding of the subject. Nonetheless, given the essay was written for an introductory course, this concern is not serious; showing broad understanding becomes more important at higher levels.

Activity 12.1 Marking a complete essay   ACTIVITY 12.1

Now it is your turn to mark an essay. The essay, which is on the popular subject of zombies, is responding to the question, 'What do our depictions of zombies tell us about ourselves?' The idea behind this question is that often when we depict creatures different from ourselves which are abhorrent, we are revealing something about ourselves. Read the essay closely and comment on each of the criteria used in the above marking sheets, keeping in mind all that has been covered in this book. Take note of reporting verbs/phrases and transition signals. Think about where the essay lies on a continuum between fail and excellent. Some thoughts are provided in the Appendix.

(Continued)

Essay question

What do our depictions of zombies tell us about ourselves?

Essay

The recent explosion of interest in zombies can clearly be seen in the numerous and diverse representations of them in current literature and film. Film and literature is often used to indicate and comment on the social mindset of the time and a closer look at these zombie illustrations highlights a reoccurring theme, that these zombies are representations of us and our current behaviours. This essay will argue that current depictions of zombies are a reflection on our behaviours and beliefs and we need to adjust these behaviours in order to survive. Through depictions of the pre-apocalyptic world in which humans are curious to the point of no return and largely consumer driven, we recognize that this behaviour leads directly to the apocalyptic world and if we don't regulate our behaviour, our downfall is inevitable. Despite these powerful inherent human characteristics, our natural human instinct to survive and overwhelming need for hope has fuelled depictions of a select few who can survive. Taking a look at these individuals however, reveals an adjustment of previous behaviours which has allowed them to endure.

   Current representations of zombies seem to hint at our belief that society needs to regulate this persisting, unregulated behaviour of searching for self-importance in order to survive (Graves 2010, p.4). Today's illustrations, such as the zombies seen in I am Legend (2007) and World War Z (2013), seem to suggest that the apocalyptic world of zombies comes about as a direct result of this behaviour of obsessing rather than fearing the unknown. This obsession is mostly due to our natural disposition towards curiosity. In particular, our lack of regulation due to overriding curiosity in regards to scientific experimentation with the unknown, through vaccines and genetic modification, which aid the progression to an unrealistic utopian society, could lead to humanity's downfall. It is tampering with genetics to enhance society, as seen by the vaccine created to cure cancer in I am Legend, which causes the viral manifestation of the zombie (2007). In other words, our obsessive rather than cautious nature overrules, we tamper and thus our actions directly lead to the creation of the zombie. Indirectly, these depictions emphasize the need for mindfulness in regards to our actions as the "growing interest in mindfulness…" directly links to "flourishing portrayals of the zombie apocalypse in contemporary societies,"(Goto-Jones 2013; Davis 1988, p.3). Thus zombies seem to be the result of our lack of mindfulness, specifically in regards to experimentation and this tells us we need to control our behaviour, become more mindful, in order to avoid disaster (Revonsuo et al 2000, p. 331–335).

While we need to regulate our curious nature and behaviours in regards to experimentation, we also need to take into consideration society as a whole. Society has progressively developed into one in which individuals are largely egotistical and consumer driven. Thus our depiction of zombies as brain-dead, emotionless beings are a direct comment on us as individuals (Rutherford 2013, p.7–8). Loudermilk's essay describes Romero's Dawn of the Dead (1978) as a direct reference to America's consumerist society by "locating the postmodern zombie historically in popular culture . . . and articulating all the while the parallels between Dawn's postmodern zombie and the North American consumer," (2003 p. 83;). Hence, it appears that a zombie apocalypse is an inevitable consequence of our current society as it increasingly becomes individualized and consumer driven with individuals only caring for themselves. While the zombie is the perfect monster for this mood it is as Rafferty suggests "a little disturbing to think that these nonhuman creatures, with their slack, gaping maws, might be serving as metaphors for actual people," (2011). The fact that even the film is set in a shopping centre redefines the zombie "so as to infect consumer identity," (Loudermilk 2003, p.83). Dawn of the Dead further indicates this idea through the protagonist Fran's questioning, "What are they doing? Why do they come here?" in regards to the shopping centre, while her boyfriend Stephen replies, "Some kind of instinct . . . memory . . . of what they used to do. This was an important place in their lives" (Bishop 2010 p.234; Dawn of the Dead 1978). By using the shopping centre as a metaphor for consumerism and directly indicating the importance of it to the humans of the past and zombies of the present, Romero emphasizes the problems with the consumerist ideals of the past and how they have impacted the present. No reasonable individual wants an apocalypse to eventuate and so by creating representations of this world, society can reflect on its actions and adjust its behaviour. It is therefore through our own depictions of zombies that we are able to comment on our existing actions in order to change them and achieve redemption.

Despite our depictions of the apocalyptic world highlighting a lack of regulation in regards to our behaviour, they also illustrate another dominant trait, our natural drive for survival. This trait has compelled depictions of a select few in society that can be saved and thus continue the race but only if they realize the problems with their curious nature in regards to experimentation and regulate consumer driven ideals. As Vidergar states, "Even if as a society we have lost a lot of belief in a positive future and instead have more of an idea of a disaster to come, we still think that we are survivors, we still want to believe that we would survive." This is a, "testament to people's desire to not only survive, but even possibly improve the world in face of a seemingly impossible situation," (Geiser 2013; Vidergar 2013 p.182–183). It is interesting that while our naturally curious nature could be our detriment, it's our instinctive nature to survive that creates depictions of post-apocalyptic survival,

(Continued)

often through curing the thing we have created. This is further illustrated in I am legend and World War Z, where a vaccine provides the savior to the human race (2007; 2013). Our depictions of zombies, which while due to our unregulated behaviour, still always seem to involve small bands of survivors fighting to continue humanity, which indicates the belief that humans are fundamentally driven by hope.

In conclusion, the present and emerging illustrations of zombies seem to indicate an overall dissatisfaction with society's current behaviour. Firstly, through depictions of individuals and their lack of regulation in regards to their own curiosity in experimentation in order to achieve utopia by tampering with the unknown. Secondly, by criticizing the consumer driven ideals of individuals by suggesting they directly relate to the downfall of society. Despite this, it seems as though another natural instinct, a need to survive, has the possibility of prevailing over our curious nature. If this trait is allowed to dominate, it could enable society to endure, but only if we recognize our faults and are willing to regulate our behaviour accordingly. Hence, our current depictions of zombies are a reflection on our current behaviour and the belief that we need to adjust our behaviour in order to ensure the survival of the human race.

References

Bishop, K 2010, 'The Idle Proletariat: Dawn of the Dead, consumer ideology, and the loss of productive labor', *The Journal of Popular Culture*, vol. 43, pp.234–248

Davis, E 1988, *Passage of darkness: The ethnobiology of the Haitian zombie*, UNC Press Books, United States

Geiser, K 2013, 'Stanford scholar explains why zombie fascination is very much alive', *Stanford News*, accessed 10 September 2015, < http://news.stanford.edu/news/2013/february/why-zombie-fascination-022013.html/>

Goto-Jones, C 2013, 'Zombie Apocalypse as Mindfulness Manifesto (after Žižek)', *Postmodern Culture*, vol. 24, no. 1.

Graves, Z 2010, *Zombies: The Complete Guide to the World of the Living Dead*, Sphere, London, United Kingdom

I am Legend 2007, DVD. Warner Brothers Pictures, United States

Loudermilk, A 2003, 'Eating "Dawn" in the Dark Zombie desire and commodified identity in George A. Romero's Dawn of the Dead', *Journal of Consumer Culture* vol. 3 no. 1 pp. 83–108

Rafferty, T 2011, 'The State of Zombie Literature: An Autopsy', *The New York Times*.

Revonsuo, A, Johanson, M, Wedlund, J, & Chaplin, J 2000, 'The Zombies Among Us,' in Rossetti Y & Revonsuo (ed.), Beyond Dissociation: Interaction Between Dissociated Implicit and Explicit Processing, John Benjamins Publishing Co, vol. 22, no. 331, pp.331–352.

Rutherford, J 2013, *Zombies*, Routledge, New York, NY

Vidergar, A B 2013, *Fictions of Destruction: Post-1945 Narrative and Disaster in the Collective Imaginary*, Stanford University, United States

World War Z 2013, DVD. Paramount Pictures, United States

Appendix: Answers to Activities

Activity 2.3

Analysis

While the student needs to clarify what they mean by the concept 'sovereign consciousness' (ideally this would occur at the beginning of the body of the essay), it is clear enough at this point that sovereign consciousness involves not only being self-aware, but being able to govern (to use the student's word) and thus modify one's self. Given this, it would be reasonable to ask, if an artificial intelligence (AI) is self-governing, then would it be possible to programme it with the core goal of philanthropy? In other words, it seems logically inconsistent that a self-governing AI could be programmed with an unmodifiable core goal. A marker may point this out; though they may wait to see the details of the student's argument as it is possible that this logical flaw can be resolved by modifying the definition of sovereign consciousness.

Activity 2.4

- **In response to Question 4**
  It is always tricky talking about truth. Among many possible objections, some might say that truth itself is a questionable concept. Not only are truths hard to pin down and at times culturally specific, sometimes people make claims about the nature of reality to oppress others; for example, many once considered it true that women were inferior to men. With these points in mind, perhaps we should be wary of being too ardent about truth.

- **In response to Question 5**
  Arguably, we can thank critical thinking for just about every scientific discovery that has ever been made. For thousands of years scientists have observed patterns in the world and used reasoning and evidence to convince themselves and others that these patterns exist. In doing this they have created knowledge. Critical thinking also arguably lies at

the heart of what we might call 'civilisation'. Wise people who observed patterns in human nature and societies developed political systems which continue to allow large amounts of people to coexist in peace. These systems include democracy and the rule of law.

- **In response to question 6**
  Some might argue that the scientific discoveries made possible by critical thinking are double edged. Many benefit the world, but others have damaged the world. Advances in technology now threaten the global environment, and the weapons we have created over the last century could potentially destroy most life on earth. Despite critical thinking playing a role in creating these problems, it is hard to blame critical thinking for them. It might be better to blame people's desire for power, or even just people's complacency. But all of this remains debatable.

Activity 3.1

Paragraph including paraphrase

While it is important for students to maintain their own voice when writing essays, too often they fail to support their opinions with sufficient evidence. Thus, while Stott (1984:50–51) is correct to encourage students to write from personal experience and to put their beliefs in their work, he does not place sufficient weight on the need to support these beliefs with compelling evidence. Many students hold largely untested beliefs and these should not be uncritically transferred into their work. It would have been preferable for Stott to say that strong personal beliefs are an excellent point from which to begin researching.

Activity 4.1

Analysis

- [1] **Approach 1** The words 'frequently encountered point' give the impression that the student is knowledgeable about the subject. However, unless some kind of evidence is provided, using such language can backfire (fortunately evidence is provided in [2]).
- [2]–[3] **Approach 2** By citing remarks by a prominent proponent of the free market, the student efficiently supports their general point. Note, however, that the student speaks about 'rights' but Abbott speaks about 'responsibilities'. The student does not deal with this subtle shift in emphasis.
- [2] **Approach 6** The reporting verb 'asserted' presages the negative evaluation that follows.

- [4] **Approaches 5 and 1** A contrasting perspective is introduced. And importantly, by touching on the perennial political debate between those who believe individuals are ultimately responsible for themselves and those who believe that structural forces reduce individual responsibility, the student is showing a broad understanding of the subject (that is, an understanding of the patterns/assumptions which underpin the subject).
- [4] **Approach 5** The neutral reporting verb, 'argues', when contrasted with the negative reporting verb used to introduce Abbott's position, presages a positive evaluation.
- [5]–[6] **Approaches 8 and 6** The student builds upon Gittins' argument and also critiques Abbott's argument.
- [6]–[11] **Approaches 8 and 6** The student makes another argument which builds upon both Gittins' and their own arguments and continues their critique of Abbott. Note how this argument clearly engages with the question. This is where you want to be at the end of your more analytic paragraphs.
- [9] **Approach 2** The student makes a claim and indicates with an in-text citation where evidence that supports the claim can be found.

Activity 5.1

Analysis

- [1] Both 'ideologies and education' are not needed. 'Education' should be enough. Also, 'Ideologies' is problematic because it is a contested term, that is, people argue about what it means.
- [2] Out of 'rules, values and stereotypes', perhaps 'rules and values' are enough. 'Stereotypes' is a subset of 'values'.
- [2] 'places where ... worse' adds little and can be removed.
- [2] With respect to 'places that ... ideologies', the idea that science fiction can encourage new actions is interesting; however, this could be more succinctly expressed.
- [4]–[5] The second and third sentences of the quotation add little to the first sentence and can be removed.

Improved version

A second function of science fiction in human development is its contribution to education. Science fiction is able to broaden people's perspectives and encourage new actions by depicting societies with unfamiliar rules and values. This is supported by Bainbridge's argument that 'Science fiction is a resource, offering ideas about possible courses of action and interpretations of reality' (1986, p. 156).

Analysis of the improved version

128 words have been reduced to 57 with very little loss of meaning. It is possible to go even further and paraphrase the Bainbridge quotation and incorporate it in the second sentence.

Activity 5.2

Dubious passage

File sharing is a thing when your given access to digital movies, songs and TV shows and when you give access to you're movies, music and TV show's, and when both of you can copy the files onto their own PC or stick. Files are shared on sites that connect users with each other so that the files can be downloaded in the blink of an eye. You can go onto a site and search and look for what you want, like TV show's and movies and download them to your PC. File sharing is illegal as it goes against copyright laws; and those doing it are acting illegally. Do they understand that its being illegal and evil and that it negatively effects producers? I think they need support.

Informal and wordy; 'occurs'
Grammar; 'you are'
The next part of the sentence is repetitive
Grammar; 'your'
Punctuation; 'shows'
Grammar; 'a'
Informal; 'computer or other storage device'
Informal; 'websites'
cliché; 'quickly'
Informal; 'is a breach of'
Punctuation; 'it is'
Informal; 'dishonest'
Avoid rhetorical questions
Questionable use of 'I'
More words needed to make meaning clear

Improved version

File sharing occurs when one allows or is allowed access to a digital collection of movies, music and TV shows. These digital files can be rapidly copied onto a computer or other storage device. Files are shared on websites that connect users with one another. File sharing is illegal as it is a breach of copyright laws. However, many people do not view it as an illegal or dishonest act, nor are they concerned about the impact on content producers. Arguably, this is a problem because if content producers do not receive revenue, content will not be produced.

Activity 6.1

Analysis

- The ambiguity in Question 1 lies in the interpretation of the word 'how'. The writer of the question intended the question to mean, 'Compare what people once thought about childhood with what they now think about childhood.' Here 'how' could be rephrased as 'in what manner'. However, many students interpreted the question to mean, 'What caused ideas about childhood to change over the centuries.' In this instance the marker accepted this second interpretation as it still allows nuanced and relevant essay.
- The ambiguity in Question 2 is more serious from the student's perspective. The problem is that the question contains two statements; thus, a student could reasonably think they had to discuss both statements. However, the writer of the question only intended students to respond to the second statement; the first statement was there to orient the question. If a student attempted to discuss both statements they could end up in a logical mess: if they disagreed with the first statement they would have trouble engaging meaningfully with the second.
- The creator of Question 3 wanted the students to analyse a particular comedic or humorous event. Students interpreted the question to be asking for a general discussion of theories of humour and comedy.

Activity 6.2

Analysis

- In sentences 3 and 4 the student indicates that they understand 'change the world' to include both world-wide change and individual change. This thoughtful modification is a good sign of independent thought.
- In sentence 7 'change' becomes 'social progression'. While it makes sense to interpret 'change' as 'social progress', this interpretation should have been explicitly made. Better might have been: 'it will discuss how comedy in fact can hinder change, when change is understood as social progress, by giving …'
- In sentence 8 'change' has become 'progress and change'. This is imprecise. Perhaps the student could have written 'social progress' if they had improved the wording of the previous sentence.

Activity 8.1

Analysis

- [1] The student begins strongly by demonstrating they are aware that the focus of the question is the limited liability company. This is implied by the question, but not explicitly stated. The student also immediately establishes that the topic is highly significant by noting the centrality of the limited liability company within the capitalist world.

- [2] The transition signal 'however' indicates that a problem is about to be introduced. The general nature of the problem is then mentioned.
- [3]–[4] The specific nature of the problem is introduced. One of the key elements of the question – the group structure of many modern companies – is incorporated. The articulation of the problem is impressive given that the problem is only implied by the question. In articulating this problem the student is demonstrating they understand the key issue contained within the question.
- [5]–[6] Here the student paraphrases the question, but in a way that links the question with the earlier parts of the orientation. Altogether, the student does an excellent job of taking ownership of the question. A strong impression of independence is generated.

Activity 8.2

Analysis

- Thesis 3 is the worst because it fails to answer the question. While the argument introduced does have some relevance to the question, the student needed to do much more to establish the relationship between the thesis and the question. In particular, they needed to mention the beach, suburbs and bush.
- Thesis 1 is the second worst because while it does engage with a part of the question, it neglects the 'to what extent' aspect of the question and thus presents a 'black and white' argument.
- Thesis 4 is the second best because it engages with every aspect of the question and makes a plausible argument. However, the argument is a little predictable.
- Thesis 2 is the best not only because it answers the question but because of its originality. It is impressive how the student differentiates between 'images' and 'ideas' and engages with the perennial pattern of ostensible changes masking underlying continuities.

Activity 8.3

Analysis

- [1] The article begins by immediately introducing the subject: Plato's ideas about women. We are also given the sense that this subject is significant: Plato's ideas about women have attracted considerable attention recently.
- [2] The significance of the subject is further established (Plato's ideas about women are radical).

- [3] In the absence of a given question, Okin must establish the problem she will address. She begins to do this in sentence [3].
- [4]–[5] Okin elaborates on the problem introduced in [3].
- [6] This sentence begins by briefly narrowing the scope (no justification is given for the decision to narrow the scope but this is not really a problem). An aim is then articulated. While aims are certainly not necessary in essay introductions, an aim is useful here because it clarifies the problem being addressed.
- [7] This is Okin's thesis.
- [8] A brief outline is provided.

Activity 9.1

Analysis

General comment: This paragraph makes some relevant points and supports these with sources. However, it is repetitive and could have been better organised. Greater depth of analysis was also possible; although this is harder to comment on if you are unfamiliar with the subject.

Comments in relation to specific rules:

- *Ensure the content of the paragraph is relevant and useful*
The content of the paragraph is relevant and useful. The topic sentence uses the language of the question to link the point being made to the question.
- *Be mindful that your paragraphs are not too short or too long*
The paragraph is a reasonable length. However, the repetition could have been removed and deeper analysis included (see below).
- *Employ the general structure of topic sentence(s) followed by elaboration*
The paragraph has this structure.
- *Include concluding sentences when appropriate*
This paragraph does not have a summative concluding sentence, but it does not need one. Instead, it concludes by providing a link with the next paragraph. This works well.
- *Ensure there is a logical flow within your paragraphs and signpost this with transition signals*
The repetition mars the logic of the paragraph. Despite this, the student uses good transition signals and also reporting verbs ('first', 'The reason', 'An example', 'However', 'And yet', 'Hobbes suggests that').
- *Be cautious when using others' words or ideas in your topic sentences*
The student's voice is strong in the topic sentence.
- *Ensure there is only one point per paragraph*
This is done. When the paragraph is in danger of introducing a new point (relief theory), it ends.

- *Avoid unnecessary repetition between and within paragraphs*
  The summaries in [2] and [6] contain similar information and so they should be combined. The analyses in sentences [4–5] and [7–8] are also similar and could be mentioned together. This would free up more words for deeper analysis. For example, an issue that could have been addressed is why the enjoyment of superiority is sometimes expressed in laughter; a lot of the time this is not the case.
- *Maintain a good balance between your voice and others' voices*
  This is done.

Activity 11.1

Modified conclusion (new material underlined)

[1] Environmental disasters, especially those caused by global warming, are an ongoing possibility. [2] In thinking about how to mitigate such disasters, it is worth considering whether the tool of humanitarian intervention is useful. [3] To this end, this essay established that there is a clear link between the violation of human rights and environmental degradation, and that given this, the 'harder' law of human rights instruments can give legal strength to environmental concerns when they are framed in a human rights perspective. [4] Thinking specifically about humanitarian intervention, it was argued that we can identify a link between the human rights violated by environmental degradation and the crimes of genocide and crimes against humanity. [5] However, as was shown, this link is highly debatable and would certainly be challenged. [6] Yet should this link be accepted, there is an argument that humanitarian intervention to prevent environmental degradation would be justified under the Responsibility to Protect doctrine, which is itself slowly moving towards acceptance as a norm of international law. [7] However, once again, problems abound, not least of which is the fact that the world's biggest polluters, who would be the natural targets of any intervention, also control the world's strongest militaries. [8] Thus, while a case can be made for humanitarian intervention on environmental grounds, such interventions are unlikely ever to eventuate.

The main modifications

- [1]–[2] A brief orientation has been added in which the problem being addressed is reintroduced and the significance of the problem is implied.
- [8] A final sentence has been added which provides a general response to the question.
- Throughout, 'concluding language' (for example, 'this essay established that') and signposting (for example, 'and given this') have been added.

Activity 12.1

The full essay is annotated below. Some corrections are made to expression and grammar. The completed marking sheet follows. The reference list is not annotated as it is reasonable.

Essay question

What do our depictions of zombies tell us about ourselves?

Essay

The recent explosion of interest in zombies can clearly be seen in the numerous and diverse representations of them in current literature and film. ~~Film and literature~~ Literature and film is often used to indicate and comment on the ~~social mindset~~ behaviours and beliefs of the time and ~~a closer look at~~ an examination of these zombie ~~illustrations~~ depictions highlights a ~~reoccurring~~ recurring theme:~~, that~~ these zombies ~~are representations of us and our current behaviours~~ represent us. This essay will argue that current depictions of zombies ~~are a reflection on our~~ reflect and critique developed societies' behaviours and beliefs and imply that these behaviours and beliefs need to change for humanity ~~we need to adjust these behaviours in order~~ to survive. Through depictions of the pre-apocalyptic world in which humans are curious to the point of no return and largely consumer driven, we recognize that this behaviour leads directly to the apocalyptic world and if we ~~don't~~ do not regulate our behaviour, our downfall is inevitable. Despite these powerful ~~inherent~~ human characteristics, ~~our natural human~~ humanity's instinct to survive and overwhelming need for hope has fuelled depictions of a select few who can survive. ~~Taking a look at~~ Examining these individuals, however, reveals an adjustment of previous behaviours which has allowed them to endure.

The significance of the subject is indicated.
Informal
The student should stick to the language of the question.
The orientation ends here. The orientation is reasonable.
This sentence is the essay's thesis. It provides a clear, albeit quite general, response to the question.
Nothing indicates that this is the beginning of the outline. This sentence repeats some of the ideas in the thesis; this is not desirable.
This is too vague.
Tautological
Tautological
This point is not obviously relevant. It is somewhat rescued by the next sentence.
Informal
This point is more relevant. The idea is that the human survivors of zombie apocalypses demonstrate the regulated behaviour lacking in pre-apocalyptic humans.

Current representations of zombies ~~seem to~~ hint at our belief that society needs to regulate ~~this~~ the persisting, unregulated behaviour of searching for self-importance in order to survive (Graves 2010, p.4). Today's illustrations, such as the zombies seen in I am Legend (2007) and World War Z (2013), ~~seem to~~ suggest that the apocalyptic world of zombies comes about as a direct result of ~~this~~ the behaviour of obsessing about rather than fearing the unknown. This obsession is mostly due to our natural disposition towards curiosity. In particular, ~~our~~ humanity's lack of regulation due to overriding curiosity in regards to scientific experimentation, ~~with the unknown~~ through vaccines and genetic modification, which aids the progression to an unrealistic utopian society, could lead to humanity's downfall. It is tampering with genetics to enhance society, as seen by the vaccine created to cure cancer in I am Legend, which causes the viral manifestation of the zombie (2007). In other words, our obsessive rather than cautious nature overrules, we tamper and thus our actions directly lead to the creation of the zombie. Indirectly, these depictions emphasize the need for mindfulness in regards to our actions as the "growing interest in mindfulness..." directly links to "flourishing portrayals of the zombie apocalypse in contemporary societies"(Goto-Jones 2013; Davis 1988, p.3). Thus zombies seem to be the result of our lack of mindfulness, specifically in regards to experimentation and this tells us we need to control our behaviour, become more mindful, in order to avoid disaster (Revonsuo et al 2000, p. 331–335).

Annotations:

- Too much hedging.
- This is too vague. Is this the same as being 'curious to the point of no return'?
- This topic sentence incorporates a paraphrase; however the student's voice remains reasonably strong.
- Italics needed.
- Is obsessing about the unknown the same as 'searching for self-importance in order to survive'? There seems to be a good point in here, but it is not being clearly expressed.
- Reasonable use of an example.
- This discussion of mindfulness is potentially a new point and could occur in a new paragraph.
- The point being made here needs to be clarified. As it stands, it seems like a tenuous link is being made.
- A page number is needed for the quotations.
- Informal
- This concluding sentence does a reasonable job of linking the material in the paragraph with the question/thesis.
- Should be 'pp'
- While the student's voice is strong in this paragraph and some interesting sources are incorporated, the arguments do not really hold together. Too many ideas and terms are introduced and not clearly explained.

While we need to regulate our curious nature and behaviours in regards to experimentation, we also need to take into consideration society as a whole. Society has ~~progressively~~ developed into one in which individuals are largely egotistical and consumer driven. <u>Thus</u> our depiction of zombies as brain-dead, emotionless beings ~~are~~ is a direct comment on us as individuals (Rutherford 2013, p.7-8). Loudermilk's essay <u>describes</u> Romero's Dawn of the Dead (1978) as a direct reference to America's consumerist society by "locating the postmodern zombie historically in popular culture... and articulating all the while the parallels between Dawn's postmodern zombie and the North American consumer" (2003 p. 83). <u>Hence</u>, it appears that a zombie apocalypse is an inevitable consequence of our current society as it increasingly becomes individualized and consumer driven with individuals only caring for themselves. While the zombie is the perfect monster for this mood it is as Rafferty suggests "a little disturbing to think that these nonhuman creatures, with their slack, gaping maws, might be serving as metaphors for actual people" (2011). The fact that even the film is set in a shopping centre redefines the zombie "so as to infect consumer identity" (Loudermilk 2003, p.83). Dawn of the Dead <u>further</u> indicates this idea through the protagonist Fran's questioning, "What are they doing? Why do they come here?" in regards to the shopping centre, while her boyfriend Stephen replies, "Some kind of instinct... memory... of what they used to do. This was an important

Strong link with previous paragraph.

Clumsy expression

Good link with the question. The first three sentences of this paragraph are the topic sentences.

Should be in reference list.

Good integration of a relevant source.

This assessment is too strong. The point is that zombies are a critique of consumer society, not that consumer society will actually create a zombie apocalypse.

Much of the remainder of this paragraph adds little to what has already been said. If the student had made their point more efficiently they could have used the extra words to make more points.

place in their lives" (Bishop 2010 p.234; Dawn of the Dead 1978). By using the shopping centre as a metaphor for consumerism and directly indicating the importance of it to the humans of the past and zombies of the present, Romero emphasizes the problems with the consumerist ideals of the past and how they have impacted the present. No reasonable individual wants an apocalypse to eventuate and so by creating representations of this world, society can reflect on its actions and adjust its behaviour. It is therefore through our own depictions of zombies that we are able to comment on our existing actions in order to change them and achieve redemption.

These concluding sentences link the material in the paragraph with the question/thesis.

~~Despite~~ While our depictions of the apocalyptic world highlight~~ing~~ a lack of regulation in regards to our behaviour, they also illustrate another dominant trait, our natural drive for survival. This trait has compelled depictions of a select few in society that can be saved and thus continue the race but only if they realize the problems with their curious nature in regards to experimentation and regulate consumer driven ideals. As Vidergar states, "Even if as a society we have lost a lot of belief in a positive future and instead have more of an idea of a disaster to come, we still think that we are survivors, we still want to believe that we would survive." This is a, "testament to people's desire to not only survive, but even possibly improve the world in face of a seemingly impossible situation" (Geiser 2013; Vidergar 2013 p.182-183). It is

While these topic sentences do help to answer the question, the paragraph could have been improved if it had begun with a modified version of the second sentence. The relevant point for the student's thesis seems to be that the depiction of survivors functions to show that survival is possible if behaviour is modified, rather than that the depiction of survivors demonstrates humanity's drive to survive.

A few more words are needed to clarify the significance of Vidergar's remarks.

interesting that while our naturally curious nature could be our detriment, ~~it's~~ it is our instinct~~ive nature~~ to survive that creates depictions of post-apocalyptic survival, often through curing the thing we have created. This is ~~further~~ illustrated in I am legend and World War Z where a vaccine provides the saviour to the human race (2007; 2013). Our depictions of zombies, which while due to our unregulated behaviour, still always seem to involve small bands of survivors fighting to continue humanity, which indicates the belief that humans are fundamentally driven by hope.

In conclusion, the present and emerging ~~illustrations~~ depictions of zombies seem to indicate an overall dissatisfaction with society's current behaviour. Firstly, through depictions of individuals and their lack of regulation in regards to their own curiosity in experimentation in order to achieve utopia by tampering with the unknown. Secondly, by criticizing the consumer driven ideals of individuals by suggesting they directly relate to the downfall of society. Despite this, it seems as though another natural instinct, a need to survive, has the possibility of prevailing over our curious nature. If this trait is allowed to dominate, it could enable society to endure, but only if we recognize our faults and are willing to regulate our behaviour accordingly. Hence, our ~~current~~ depictions of zombies are a reflection on our current behaviour and the belief that we need to adjust our behaviour in order to ensure the survival of the human race.

Clumsy.

While this point is related to the topic sentences, it is not obvious how it develops them. Greater precision is needed.

Good use of examples.

These dates should come after each movie.

This concluding sentence relates more to the first sentence in this paragraph than the second. Because of this, while it does answer the question, once again the thesis is not well supported.

Writing 'In conclusion' is fine here. Note the student does not use past simple or present perfect tense in the conclusion; doing so would have made the conclusion sound more like a conclusion.

A bit wordy.

Some caution is shown. Maybe this is not necessary at this point.

The conclusion begins with a more general version of the essay's thesis. This works well.

This is not a sentence.

This is also not a sentence.

This point is better expressed than it was in the introduction or in the third body paragraph.

Nice clear finish.

Marking sheet

Is the introduction well constructed? • Orientation • Thesis • Outline	While the introduction introduces the subject, presents a general argument and provides an outline, it is not entirely convincing. The problems lie mostly in the outline. The first sentence in the outline is somewhat repetitive, and it is not immediately obvious how the second sentence supports the thesis.
Is the body well constructed? • General logic (essay's skeleton) • Structure of individual paragraphs	The essay has a largely clear general logic; although this could have been improved if some of the topic sentences had been clearer. Individual paragraphs are somewhat well structured. We see reasonably ordered transitions from topic sentences to examples to analysis to concluding sentences. However, the elaboration on the topic sentences is not always clear and repetition sometimes creeps in.
Is the conclusion well constructed? • Summary • Thesis restated	The conclusion is well constructed but it could have been better expressed.
Is knowledge and understanding of the subject demonstrated?	The student has found a number of good-quality sources and illustrates their points with reasonable examples. However, the student only uses their sources to make largely straightforward points and never really engages with them in a critical manner (comparing, contrasting, evaluating). Thus, while some knowledge is demonstrated, understanding is only superficial.
Are the sources well integrated?	For the most part the sources are well integrated. At times better introducing and more analysis are needed.
Is the referencing correct? • In-text referencing • Reference list	For the in-text referencing, sometimes two citations appear in the brackets and it is not clear which part of the sentence each belongs to. The reference list is well constructed.
Is critical thinking demonstrated?	The student's voice is clearly present in this essay; however, the student's reasoning is not always convincing. Also, the response does not explore the complexities of the subject in a substantial manner.
Is there a sustained and convincing engagement with the question?	The engagement with the question is largely sustained. And while the third point does not support the thesis as well as it might have, the student's response is generally convincing. The response would have been more convincing if a less superficial approach had been taken.

Is the expression appropriate? • Level of formality • Grammar	There is some informality. Clichés and tautologies are also present. The student's writing is also sometimes too wordy and fails to stick to key terms, making the meaning at times hard to follow. Grammar could have been improved.
General comment	This is an average essay. The general structure is largely coherent and individual paragraphs are in parts well constructed. A plausible thesis is introduced in the introduction; however, the argument in the thesis is not quite sustained throughout the essay. A number of good sources are included; however, the sources are rarely explored in any depth (there is very little comparing, contrasting or evaluating). The student's voice is reasonably strong, but the response remains somewhat superficial. Both expression and grammar could have been improved.

Sources Consulted

Beer, D. (2014). *Punk sociology*. Basingstoke: Palgrave Macmillan.

Butler, J. (1999). A 'bad writer' writes back. *The New York Times*, 20 March. http://query.nytimes.com/gst/fullpage. html?res=950CE5D61531F933A15750 C0A96F958260.

Department of Life Sciences. (2014). *Marking criteria & feedback forms 2014–15*. London: Imperial College London.

Department of Philosophy. (2016). *Marking criteria and procedures*. York: The University of York.

Department of Psychology (2015). *Research Paper Rubric*. New South Wales: Macquarie University.

Dutton, D. (n.d.). *The bad writing contest, press releases 1996–1998*. http://denisdutton.com/bad_writing.htm.

Faculty of Arts and Humanities. (2016). *Undergraduate generic marking criteria*. London: King's College London.

Faculty of Law. (2015). *Marks and grades*. Auckland: University of Auckland.

Faculty of Modern and Medieval Languages. (2015). *Examination by long essay*. Cambridge: The University of Cambridge. http://www.mml.cam.ac.uk/undergraduates/marking.

Greetham, B. (2013). *How to Write Better Essays*. Basingstoke: Palgrave Macmillan.

Hurley, M. M., Dennett, D. C., & Adams Jr., R. B. (2011). *Inside jokes: using humor to reverse-engineer the mind*. Massachusetts and London: The MIT Press.

King's College London. (2016). *Undergraduate generic marking criteria*. London.

Okin, S. M. (1977). Philosopher queens and private wives: Plato on women and the family. *Philosophy and Public Affairs*, 6(4), pp. 345–369.

Philosophy and Literature [Journal]. (2016). *Author guidelines*. https://www.press.jhu.edu/journals/philosophy_and_literature/guidelines.html.

Research School of Management. (2015). *Course description: Managing across cultures*. Canberra: Australian National University.

School of English. (2015). *Creative and Critical Writing Assessment Criteria for Written Work*. Sussex: University of Sussex.

School of Modern Languages. (2016). *Generic Marking Criteria*. Bristol: The University of Bristol.

School of Philosophy, Psychology and Language Sciences. (2014). *Course guide: Morality and Value*. Edinburgh: The University of Edinburgh.

School of Social Sciences. (2015). *Research paper rubric*. New South Wales: University of New South Wales.

Stott, B. (1984). *Write to the point and feel better about your writing*. New York: Anchor Press/Doubleday.

University of Exeter. (2014). *Generic university assessment criteria for taught programmes: guidance notes for staff*. http://as.exeter.ac.uk/academic-policy-standards/tqa-manual/lts/genericassessment/.

University of Liverpool. (2016). *Code of practice on assessment*. https://www. liverpool.ac.uk/media/livacuk/tqsd/code-of-practice-on-assessment/ appendix_A_2011-12_cop_assess.pdf.

University of New England. (2016). *Academic Writing*. http://learninghub.une.edu. au/tlc/aso/aso-online/academic-writing/.

University of New South Wales (2016). *Academic Integrity and Plagiarism*. https:// student.unsw.edu.au/plagiarism.

University of Oxford. (2016). *Plagiarism*. https://www.ox.ac.uk/students/academic/ guidance/skills/plagiarism?wssl=1.

Wikipedia. (2016). *Definitions of science fiction*. https://en.wikipedia.org/wiki/ Definitions_of_science_fiction.

Index